P9-DJU-787

A Gift from America

The First 50 Years of CARE

DAVID MORRIS

LONGSTREET PRESS
Atlanta, Georgia

Published by
LONGSTREET PRESS, INC.
A subsidiary of Cox Newspapers,
A subsidiary of Cox Enterprises, Inc.
2140 Newmarket Parkway, Suite 118
Marietta, GA 30067

Text copyright © 1996 CARE
Photographs copyright © 1996 CARE,
except where otherwise indicated.
All rights reserved. No part of this book
may be reproduced in any form or by any
means without the prior written permission
of the Publisher, excepting brief quotations
used in connection with reviews, written
specifically for inclusion in a magazine or
newspaper.

Printed in the United States of America
1st printing, 1996
Library of Congress Catalog Card
Number: 95-82235
ISBN: 1-56352-285-3

Cover photo: *Regine Binet of Bayeux,
France, a town not far from the Normandy
invasion beaches, receives a CARE Package
in 1946—a gift from an American she had
never met.* (CARE photo)
Title page: *Sudan*
Pages ii—iii: *Bangladesh*
Page vi: *Niger* (CARE photos by Rudolph
von Bernuth)
Back cover photo: *A CARE health worker
counsels a young mother in Bangladesh, one
of 66 developing and emerging nations where
CARE works today.* (CARE photo by
Shahidul Alam)

FIFTY

CARE

YEARS

CARE
151 Ellis St.
Atlanta, GA 30303
404-681-2552
info@care.org
www.care.org

CARE and the CARE Package are registered
trademarks of the Cooperative for Assistance
and Relief Everywhere.

Jacket and book design by Jill Dible

Electronic film prep and separations by
Advertising Technologies, Inc., Atlanta, GA

Peru *(Photo © 1993 by J. F. Housel)*

CONTENTS

INTRODUCTION

THE WORDS AND PICTURES THAT MAKE UP THIS VOLUME ARE A CHRONICLE OF NOT ONLY AN ORGANIZATION BUT AN AMERICAN MOVEMENT THAT BEGAN AFTER WORLD WAR II AND HAS CONTINUED, SOMETIMES AMID RANCOROUS DEBATE, TO THIS DAY. THAT MOVEMENT—TOWARD EVER-GREATER POLITICAL, CULTURAL AND PERSONAL ENGAGEMENT WITH THE REST OF THE WORLD—IS REFLECTED IN THE HISTORY AND GROWTH OF CARE, AMERICA'S FIRST LARGE-SCALE INTERNATIONAL CHARITY AND THE SUBJECT OF THIS BOOK.

In a very real sense, CARE, which emerged in response to World War II, became the humanitarian manifestation of America's leadership role in the postwar world. If the conflict and its aftermath convinced Americans that the world needed their help, then CARE gave them a way to act on that belief.

They acted even as the politicians agonized, using CARE to send millions of dollars in assistance to postwar Europe before the Truman administration's Marshall Plan was ever conceived. Over the next five decades, CARE became a virtual brand name for American generosity around the world. Some 35 million Americans have contributed to CARE and transformed it from a package-delivery service into the world's largest private relief and development organization.

Today's CARE has grown far beyond its American roots. Ten other industrialized nations have formed their own CAREs, transforming the concept of helping people overseas into a global movement known as CARE International. But even as CARE has grown and globalized, some Americans are backing away from the responsibility that comes with leadership and advocating a withdrawal from world affairs.

The timing of renewed isolationism is particularly ironic considering the enormous social and economic progress that has been made since the end of World War II—an era of unprecedented global engagement not only by the United States but by other industrialized nations as well. Despite the accounts of famine, disease and general calamity that dominate the way the media looks at the developing world, the fact is that conditions in most of these countries have dramatically improved in the postwar era. Life expectancy is on the rise almost everywhere. Increased access to clean water and the widespread availability of vaccines, oral-rehydration therapy and other low-tech health interventions have helped slash infant mortality. Most infectious diseases are coming under control in developing countries as they did in the industrialized world a generation or two ago. Since 1965,

average daily caloric intake has risen in all major regions of the world and in all but the poorest of countries. Meanwhile, successful development has allowed South Korea, Hong Kong, Chile and other places where CARE once worked to emerge as full-fledged participants in the world economy.

Americans should feel good about this progress, and not only because it means that other human beings have been able to live better and more productive lives. They should feel good because in helping others, Americans have helped themselves. Increased prosperity in the developing world has created more demand for American products, and U.S. exports to developing countries have more than doubled in the last 10 years. Economists estimate that exports to developing countries alone account for some two million American jobs, a statistic that merely underlines the fact that we do not live in the world alone, but are part of an ever-expanding web of global interdependence in which the actions of one entity—be it a government, a corporation, an organization or an individual—can be felt far away, and in ways once never imagined.

Since the beginning of CARE, people in the United States have made individual decisions to help—decisions that, through CARE, translated into positive changes in the lives of people across the world. These changes include higher incomes thanks to microloans for the creation or expansion of small businesses; better health and nutrition thanks to feeding programs, new agricultural techniques and greater access to clean water and sanitation; and, for victims of war and natural disaster, hope for the future thanks to CARE's emergency relief programs.

Each of the people whom CARE has helped over the last half century now has a connection with someone far away who made a decision to reach out across borders and cultural divides. Those connections extend between CARE Package senders and recipients; between wealthy corporations and tiny Andean villages; between a garden club in Sioux City, Iowa, and a poor family in Bangladesh; between every person who sat down to write a check to CARE and every person—from a starving housewife in postwar Germany to a rain-soaked Rwandan refugee—who subsequently benefited from that action.

CARE was the first charitable organization to promote such connections on a global scale. Thanks to a mass-marketing effort that made the term "CARE Package" a house-

hold word, CARE brought the plight of the world's most afflicted people to Americans' attention for the first time and told them they could do something about it. One billion people in 125 countries have been touched by America's response to CARE's call, and it is a response worthy of recognition.

That's where this book comes in. It's a photographic record of 50 years of CARE's work throughout the world, culled from photo archives that document the turning-point events of a half century: the Berlin Airlift, the Korean conflict, the Hungarian uprising, the Vietnam War, the Cambodian refugee crisis, the Somalian famine, the Rwandan genocide, the war in Bosnia. In all these crises, CARE has been on the scene, even as it worked quietly and with less fanfare in other parts of the world. Wherever it has worked, CARE's employees and others have recorded the organization's efforts in hundreds of thousands of photos, just a few of which are reproduced here. They are emblematic of the progress that can take place when people care about one another and work together to solve problems. Even more, they are a testament to human dignity and its power to triumph over all evils and all obstacles. Finally, this book is a tribute to the people who not only believe the future can be better but are making it happen every day: CARE's donors, volunteers, board members, staff and partners overseas.

A Gift from America

The First 50 Years of CARE

Making A Promise

French workers and officials welcome the first shipment of CARE Packages at Le Havre on May 11, 1946. *(CARE photo)*

For people who did not experience it themselves, the suffering and privation wrought by World War II is impossible to imagine. By August 1945, when the conflict came to its bitter end, much of Europe and Asia lay in ruins. Some 30 million people had perished, and in Europe alone the war had created 13 million refugees.

Even those who remained in their homes faced a grim struggle to survive. While once well-to-do families ate grass for sustenance and chopped furniture for firewood, a violent black market undermined governmental food-rationing efforts. It was a desperate situation, and Americans were desperate to help.

But assistance was difficult to render. The absence of reliable postal services in Europe, the possibility of theft and the high cost of shipping combined to thwart early attempts at person-to-person help.

Two men, drawing inspiration from a government program to assist victims of World War I, envisioned a new organization that would fill the void. Approaching a consortium of 22 American charities, Arthur Ringland and Dr. Lincoln Clark proposed a private, nonprofit corporation to funnel food packages from individuals and families in the United States to friends and loved ones in Europe. After months of planning, the charities agreed to support the venture, and on November 27, 1945, they created the Cooperative for American Remittances to Europe.

The fledgling organization had a clear mission, but scant resources. Yet even as CARE was looking for office space in New York, the answer to its initial problem was sitting in a warehouse in the Philippines. There, millions of U.S. Army ration packs had been stored for the invasion of Japan. In an ironic footnote to the dawn of the nuclear age, America's decision to drop the atom bomb created a massive inventory problem that gave rise to the ultimate symbol of American generosity—the CARE Package.

After months of battling various government agencies for the approval to purchase the surplus rations, CARE finally took possession of some 2.8 million "10-in-one" packages in early 1946. Each contained enough food to feed 10 men for a day, or one man for 10 days. The fare, as any old soldier will tell you, was simple—canned meat, dried milk, raisins, chocolate and even cigarettes. (One group on the CARE Board wanted to remove the cigarettes, but it was quite impossible to open 2.8 million packages and reseal them. Many recipients used them as an alternate currency, trading them for food, clothing and medicine.) For a world in the midst of a global food shortage, and for American families eager to send food to friends and relatives in Europe, the CARE Package offered the hope of better times ahead.

By the time the CARE Package went on sale in the spring of 1946, many private companies were already selling food parcels for delivery to Europe. But many of these companies were fraudulent, expensive and offered no guarantee of delivery. Alternatively, thousands of Americans were packing and mailing their own food parcels, but delivery was far from assured, as the battered postal systems of Europe struggled against theft and corruption. CARE, with America's leading charitable, labor and church groups on its board, promised guaranteed delivery and a signed receipt—or your money back. Guaranteed delivery was a formidable undertaking in countries whose roads, bridges, railways and postal services lay in ruins.

To meet the challenge, CARE sent Dr. Clark to Europe to sign agreements with governments and to forge partnerships with local groups who could help ensure deliveries. At the same time, CARE began hiring an eclectic mix of adventurers who would serve as the organization's first mission chiefs: former journalists, soldiers, labor leaders, foreign-service officers and religious officials.

Just six months after the agency's incorporation, on May 11, 1946, the mammoth efforts bore fruit. Dr. Clark, exhausted from six months of travel, supervised delivery of the first CARE Packages to grateful recipients in Le Havre, a battered port city in Normandy. The landing grounds of D-Day had become the beachhead of a new kind of invasion—an inundation of American compassion that came in a plain brown box.

ABOVE: Negotiating a pathway through a blasted landscape, this German family was one of millions struggling to survive in the immediate aftermath of World War II in Europe. *(CARE photo)*

LEFT: Years after the last bomb was dropped, people across the Continent eked out an existence under appalling conditions. Here, German children play in front of their ruined home in 1946. *(CARE photo)*

ABOVE: Children, like these in Germany showing their worn-out shoes, suffered some of the war's worst deprivation. *(CARE photo)*

LEFT: Six years of fighting had exacted a terrible toll, not only in property but in lives. *(CARE photo)*

Paul Comly French, appointed CARE's general manager in 1946, traveled to Europe to survey the devastation and recommend courses of action. *(CARE photo)*

ABOVE: In the United States, a fledgling relief organization, the Cooperative for American Remittances to Europe, made plans at its New York offices to harness American generosity on behalf of war victims overseas. At the head of the table is Wallace J. Campbell, now CARE's chairman emeritus.
(CARE photo)

ES, FRIDAY, NOVEMBER 30, 1945.

COOPERATIVE AIDS OVERSEAS RELIEF

Donald M. Nelson Heads 'World Mail-Order House' Formed to Speed Food Supplies

The formation by twenty-two agencies of a cooperative for the distribution of relief packages overseas was announced yesterday by Donald M. Nelson, president of the Society of Independent Motion Picture Producers and former head of the War Production Board, who has been named as its executive director. He disclosed plans for a confer-

Morrison, British Labor Le To Teach Opposition to O

By Wireless to THE NEW YORK

LONDON, Nov. 29 — Herbert positi
Morrison, Lord President of the oppo
Council and former Prime Minister debat
Churchill's political foe, told the the
Opposition today how it should for
oppose. The lecture appeared in ject
the Labor party's fortnightly
Labor Press Service twenty-four pos
hours after Mr. Churchill's power- sil
ful attack on the Government.

"Were it not for the fact that an o
I might be misunderstood, I am o
very tempted to offer His Majes-
ty's Opposition a private session
in a House of Commons committee
room to give them good counsel
and guidance in the execution of
its duties," Mr. Morrison said.

ABOVE: Publicity from such publications as *The New York Times* helped make the American people aware of CARE and its plans to reach out to the needy. This story appeared on November 30, 1945, after CARE was officially founded. Ironically, Nelson, a prominent business leader recruited to lead CARE, quit after a month on the job, convinced that the organization would never succeed.

CHAPTER ONE

ABOVE: CARE executives Dr. Lincoln Clark (left) and Murray Lincoln inspect the contents of one of the original 10-in-one army ration packs that became the first CARE Packages. Designed for soldiers, the packages included such staples as canned meat, butter and dried milk, but also specialty items like real coffee and chocolate that Europeans hadn't seen since before the war. One singularly American item that some Europeans didn't know what to make of was chewing gum; CARE's mission director in Warsaw reported that at least one enterprising Pole used it to flavor vodka. *(CARE photo)*

RIGHT: CARE workers in the main shipping plant in Philadelphia worked around the clock to keep up with orders. *(CARE photo)*

ABOVE: CARE employees in New York dispatch packages for Europe. CARE's early staff in New York included dozens of European refugees whose language skills and knowledge of specific cities and even streets helped clarify orders. Many viewed CARE as their personal way of rebuilding the countries they had fled, and brought a zeal and determination to their work that helped the organization survive a turbulent first year. *(CARE photo)*

ABOVE: Encouraging the American people to support CARE, President Harry S. Truman became one of the organization's first donors when he purchased 100 CARE Packages for Europe in May 1946. President Truman is shown here giving a check to CARE's first executive director, General William N. Haskell. *(CARE photo)*

Most CARE Packages were shipped from the port of Philadelphia. *(CARE photo)*

The first shipment of CARE Packages, greeted by CARE cofounder Dr. Lincoln Clark (left), arrived aboard the *American Traveler* at Le Havre, France, in May 1946. Of the city and people of Le Havre, Clark wrote: "Block after block does not have a building standing. Thousands were made homeless and injured and lost their jobs....The major difficulty is the loss of the breadwinner by death or disability. [But] I distinctly had the impression that all of the...families I visited will somehow get back on their feet. *They were all incredulous to be receiving a package....*" *(CARE photo)*

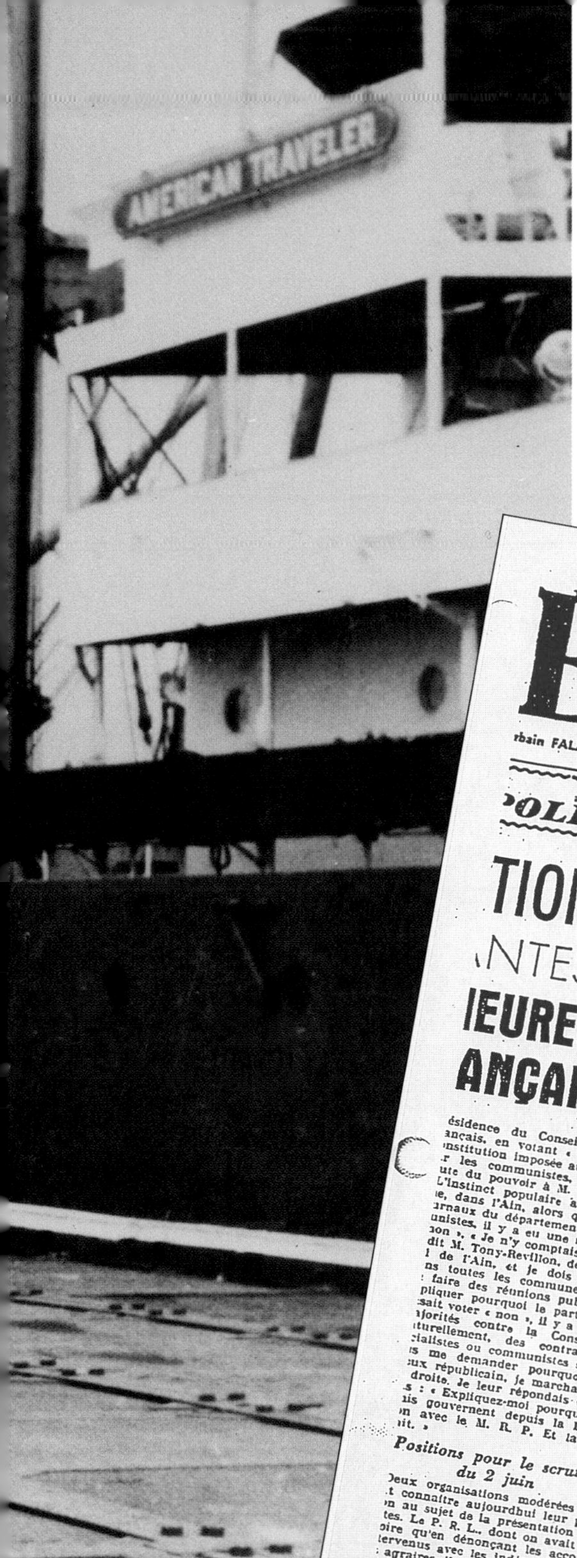

BELOW: The *Havre Eclair* announced the shipment in a front-page article reproduced here. Clark noted that the volatile French press was kind to CARE: The Catholic papers played up CARE's official blessing from the pope, the Communist journal noted CARE's close ties to the American labor movement and the conservative press admired its businesslike methods and partnership with a French cooperative business group. "CARE is everything to all people," he noted in a letter.

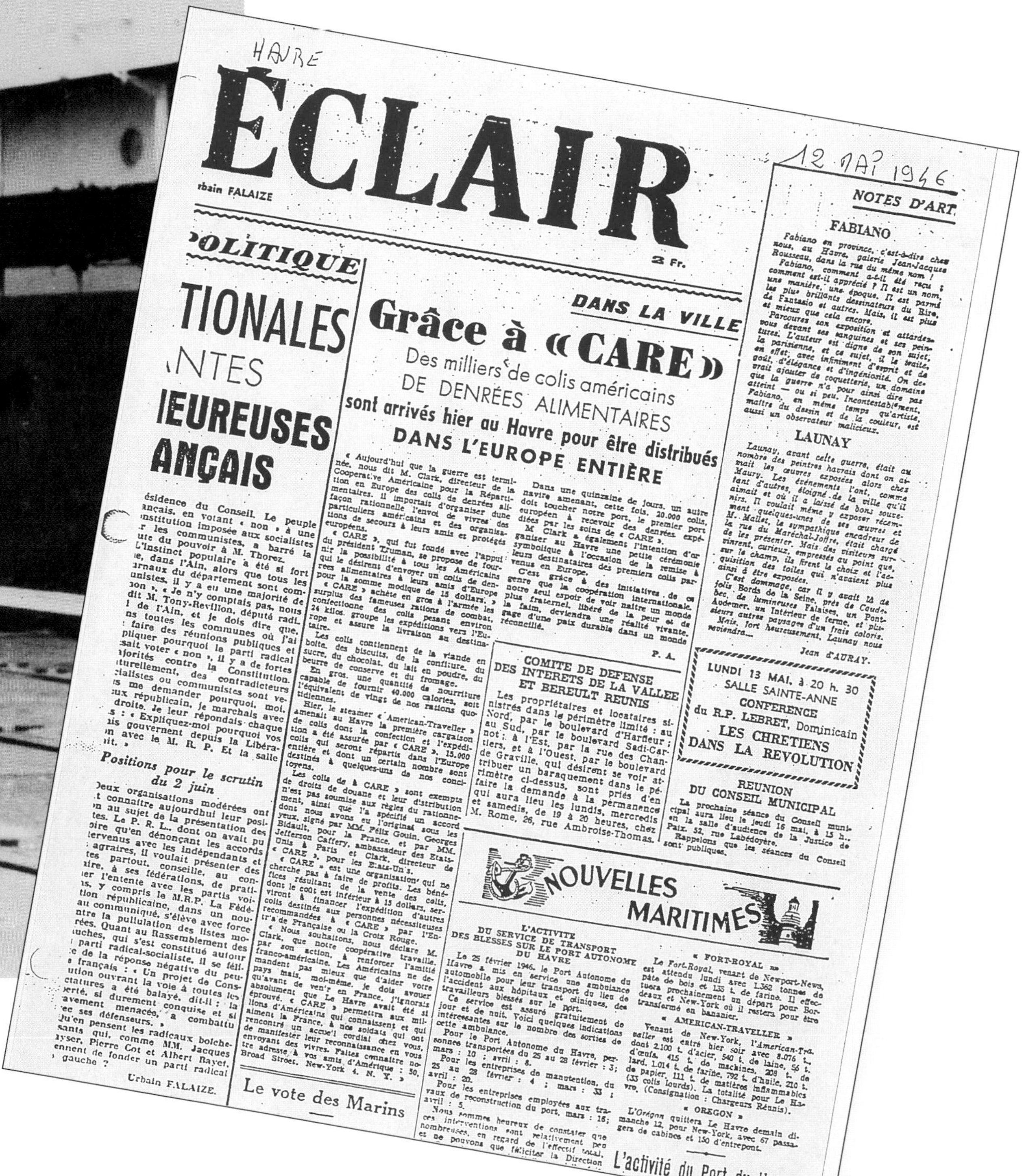

HAVRE

ECLAIR

12 MAI 1946

2 Fr.

DANS LA VILLE

Grâce à « CARE »

Des milliers de colis américains DE DENRÉES ALIMENTAIRES sont arrivés hier au Havre pour être distribués DANS L'EUROPE ENTIÈRE

« Aujourd'hui que la guerre est terminée, nous dit M. Clark, directeur de la Coopérative Américaine pour la Répartition en Europe des colis de denrées alimentaires, il importait d'organiser d'une façon rationnelle l'envoi de vivres des particuliers américains et des organisations de secours à leurs amis et protégés européens.

« CARE », qui fut fondé avec l'appui du président Truman, se propose de fournir la possibilité à tous les Américains qui le désirent d'envoyer un colis de denrées alimentaires à leurs amis d'Europe pour la somme modique de 15 dollars. »

« CARE » achète en gros à l'armée les surplus des fameuses rations de combat, confectionne des colis pesant environ 24 kilos, groupe les expéditions vers l'Europe et assure la livraison au destinataire.

Les colis contiennent de la viande en boîte, des biscuits, de la confiture, du sucre, du chocolat, du lait en poudre, du beurre de conserve et du fromage.

En gros, une quantité de nourriture capable de fournir 40.000 calories, soit l'équivalent de vingt de nos rations quotidiennes.

Hier, le steamer « American-Traveller » amenait au Havre la première cargaison de colis dont la confection et l'expédition a été assurée par « CARE ». 15.000 colis qui seront répartis dans l'Europe entière et dont un certain nombre sont destinés à quelques-uns de nos concitoyens.

Les colis de « CARE » sont exempts de droits de douane et leur distribution n'est pas soumise aux règles du rationnement, ainsi que l'a spécifié un accord dont nous avons eu l'original sous les yeux, signé par MM. Félix Gouin, Georges Bidault, pour la France, et par MM. Jefferson Caffery, ambassadeur des Etats-Unis à Paris et Clark, directeur de « CARE », pour les Etats-Unis.

« CARE » est une organisation qui ne cherche pas à faire de profits. Les bénéfices résultant de la vente des colis, dont le coût est inférieur à 15 dollars, serviront à financer l'expédition d'autres colis destinés aux personnes nécessiteuses recommandées à « CARE » par l'Entr'aide Française ou la Croix Rouge.

« Nous souhaitons, nous déclare M. Clark, que notre coopérative travaille, par son action, à renforcer l'amitié franco-américaine. Les Américains ne demandent pas mieux que d'aider votre pays mais, moi-même, je dois avouer qu'avant de venir en France, j'ignorais absolument que Le Havre avait été si éprouvé. « CARE » permettra aux millions d'Américains qui connaissent et qui aiment la France, à nos soldats qui ont rencontré un accueil cordial chez vous, de manifester leur reconnaissance en vous envoyant des vivres. Faites connaître notre adresse à vos amis d'Amérique : 50, Broad Street, New-York 4, N. Y. »

Dans une quinzaine de jours, un autre navire amenant, cette fois, 20.000 colis, doit toucher notre port, le premier port européen à recevoir des denrées expédiées par les soins de « CARE ».

M. Clark a également l'intention d'organiser au Havre une petite cérémonie symbolique à l'occasion de la remise à leurs destinataires des premiers colis parvenus en Europe.

C'est grâce à des initiatives de ce genre que la coopération internationale, notre seul espoir de voir naître un monde plus fraternel, libéré de la peur et de la faim, deviendra une réalité vivante, gage d'une paix durable dans un monde réconcilié.

P. A.

POLITIQUE

TIONALES

NTES

IEUREUSES

ANÇAIS

Positions pour le scrutin du 2 juin

Urbain FALAIZE.

NOTES D'ART

FABIANO

LAUNAY

Jean d'AURAY.

LUNDI 13 MAI, à 20 h. 30
SALLE SAINTE-ANNE
CONFERENCE
du R.P. LEBRET, Dominicain
LES CHRETIENS DANS LA REVOLUTION

REUNION DU CONSEIL MUNICIPAL

COMITE DE DEFENSE DES INTERETS DE LA VALLEE ET BEREULT REUNIS

NOUVELLES MARITIMES

L'ACTIVITE DU SERVICE DE TRANSPORT DES BLESSES SUR LE PORT AUTONOME DU HAVRE

« FORT-ROYAL »

« AMERICAN-TRAVELLER »

« OREGON »

Le vote des Marins

L'activité du Port du Havre

LEFT: In spite of many obstacles, CARE Packages kept arriving in Europe by the thousands, including these being unloaded in Naples, Italy. By early 1947, the original 10-in-ones were exhausted, and CARE began designing its own packages, including ones with tools, cloth and other goods. After a difficult first year, in which sales were slow at times, the arrival of this new CARE Package—along with a much vaunted "businesslike" approach to charity and a healthy dose of publicity—helped CARE burst onto the national scene in 1947 and make the CARE Package a part of American history. *(CARE photo)*

RIGHT: The first shipment of CARE Packages arrives in the rail yards of Vienna.
(CARE photo)

LEFT: A Dutch postcard thanks Americans for their generosity.

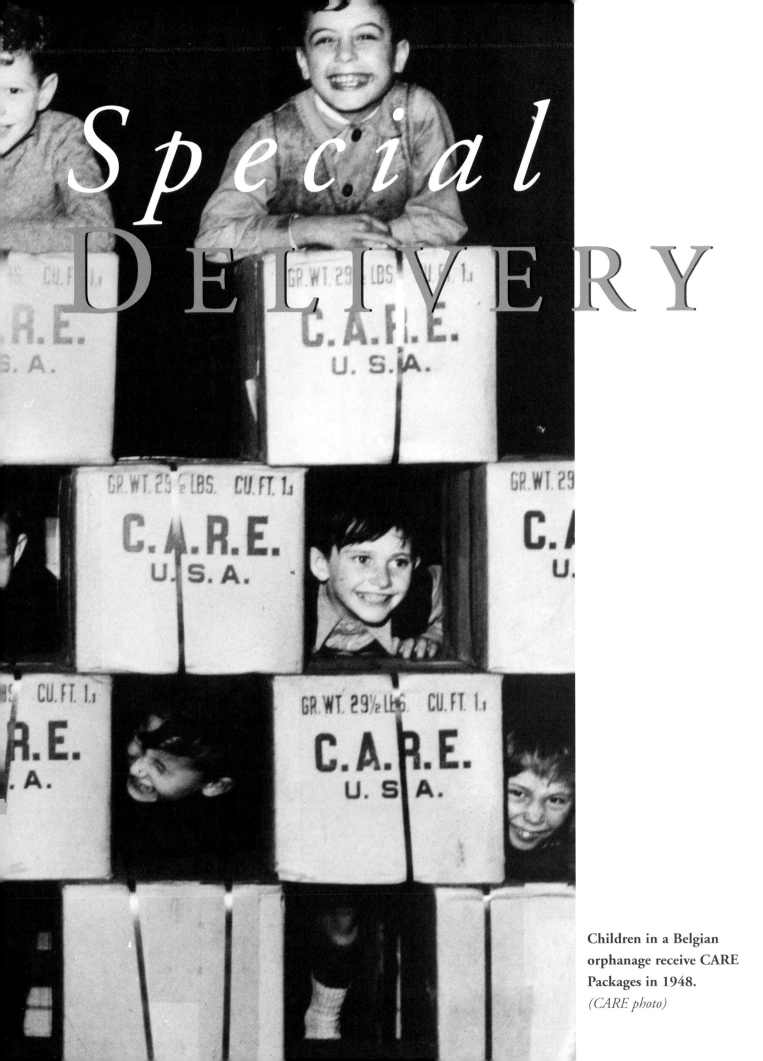

Special
DELIVERY

Children in a Belgian orphanage receive CARE Packages in 1948.
(CARE photo)

Before CARE was even a year old, an order processor in the agency's headquarters in lower Manhattan opened a piece of mail that would fundamentally change the organization and its mission within a few months' time. It was a simple order for a CARE Package, not unlike the thousands that had already been received. But instead of designating a specific recipient—say, Uncle Giuseppe in Naples—and providing a specific address, the donor wrote simply: "For a hungry person in Europe."

CARE's founders envisioned the agency as a temporary vehicle for Americans to send food to friends and family in Europe. The American public had quite another idea, and that first "undesignated" order was followed by hundreds, then thousands, then tens of thousands more.

This anonymous generosity took CARE by surprise. But the founders soon realized that the agency had to broaden its scope and become not just a link between Americans and their loved ones overseas but between Americans and the world's poor.

Even as this fundamental shift was happening, hundreds of thousands of CARE Packages were flooding into Europe, and CARE's mission chiefs worked around the clock to keep shipments moving over battered transportation systems. In 1946, despite slow initial sales, CARE delivered nearly one million packages, most after the price was lowered from $15 to $10. In 1947, the figure jumped to 2.6 million, as CARE introduced modern sales and marketing methods and benefited from an enormous tide of favorable publicity. Americans could place orders at railway stations, Macy's stores and CARE offices in major cities, or through dozens of civic and religious groups.

In the years that followed, CARE Packages played a key role in the recovery of Europe, becoming a grassroots, person-to-person version of the Marshall Plan. Soon, CARE exhausted its army-surplus stocks and designed its own packages, which included not only food but tools, cloth, medicine and, later, books. And as Europe recovered, CARE expanded into Asia, Latin America and Africa.

Eventually, more than 100 million CARE Packages would be delivered to people in need. Wherever they went, the packages shared a common trait: They were the gifts of Americans who saw CARE as the best way to reach out to people in need. The recipients, many of them citizens of countries with which the United States had been at war, were often incredulous that an American they had never met would send them aid and comfort. One young German, Klaus Putter, recalled that he and his friends refused at first to believe the package contained food. Fearing it was booby-trapped, they treated it gingerly for days before one of them pronounced: "I think I have the answer. These Americans are just different. They want to help those in need."

It was the sort of unselfish compassion that would distinguish Americans in the years following the war. Using a sturdy cardboard box as their vehicle, Americans helped turn the CARE Package into a cultural icon, a symbol of generosity worldwide and a part of the American vernacular known to any college student who has ever received a box of cookies from home.

CARE supporters are continuing that movement today, even though the familiar box has largely been replaced by a "CARE Package" encompassing a wide variety of relief and development programs. But the broader mission of CARE remains true to the spirit that inspired Americans in 1946 to look beyond their own families, communities and circle of friends, and embrace a commitment to helping anyone in need—regardless of where they lived, how they worshiped, what government they lived under or what ethnic group they belonged to. The CARE Package was, and is, universal.

A Greek woman prepares a meal for her orphaned grandson. *(CARE photo)*

What It Meant to Get a CARE Package

Early CARE Package recipients were often incredulous that someone they had never met was sending them a gift. After six years of war, compassion came as a shock, and it left its mark on many recipients. Today, many CARE donors in the U.S. and Europe are former package recipients. Here are some of their memories, in their own words:

"Those CARE Packages were incredible. My parents described them as treasure troves. When absolutely everything is gone, you've lost every shred of clothing, food, furniture, belongings, to a war, and something comes in the mail like that—that has chocolate in it, coffee, powdered milk, all these kinds of things—those were special days and special times."

— ROBERT KOVACEVICH, born to Yugoslav refugees in a displaced persons camp after the war.

TOP: Robert Kovacevich, 1948
LEFT: Robert Kovacevich, with his son, today.

A German amputee rolls his package home in a wheelchair. Germany received more CARE Packages than any nation in Europe. An estimated 40 million Germans—two-thirds of the population—benefited. *(CARE photo)*

ABOVE: British workmen unload packages in 1949. With chronic food shortages and an active black market, theft was a constant threat. In Germany, large rail shipments were accompanied by armed guards; even then they were occasionally attacked. *(CARE photo)*

LEFT AND RIGHT: As stocks of surplus army rations ran low, CARE began assembling its own food packages for the needy, emphasizing more staples like flour and butter and fewer prepared foods. As this 1947 photo (left) from Britain shows, the packages contained brand-name items from companies that remain familiar today: Fleischmann's, Swanson's, Hunt's and Tetley, among others. Packages were customized to meet the special tastes and dietary requirements of various countries and peoples; tea, for example, was substituted for coffee in British packages. Cigarettes and chewing gum, popular items in the army ration packs for their value on the black market, were eliminated from the new packages to make way for nutritious items. *(CARE photo)*

ABOVE: In northern Finland, CARE turned to a reliable form of local transport to help ensure delivery: reindeer. Because CARE guaranteed delivery, it went to great lengths—and often creative means—to move packages. CARE Packages traveled by elephant in Ceylon, on camelback in Pakistan, in open boats to the outer isles of the Hebrides and via mule train into remote Greek villages. *(CARE photo)*

LEFT: A CARE Package sleigh ride in Poland, 1948.

(CARE photo)

An American soldier helps deliver CARE Packages in Germany. Many decommissioned soldiers sent CARE Packages to sweethearts in Europe after returning to the United States. *(CARE photo)*

Children leading lives of want and deprivation received food, clothing and, above all, encouragement from CARE Packages. Here, girls in Italy sort through a package in 1947. *(CARE photo)*

ABOVE: This little Bulgarian girl, whose father was killed in the war and whose mother was desperately ill, managed a smile upon receipt of a 22-pound box of food sent by an American donor for $10. *(CARE photo)*

ABOVE: An Italian war orphan samples the items in a CARE Package at the Little House of Saint Anthony in Rome, 1948. *(CARE photo)*

"I don't think anyone who has not experienced it can ever imagine what it was like when a CARE Package arrived. It added the one bit of color, of happiness."

— EDITH WILLIAMS, who received CARE Packages in Germany in 1946 after walking 600 kilometers to be reunited with her family.

Edith Williams, 1946

Edith Williams, today

ABOVE: Paul Comly French, who became executive director of CARE in 1947, visits with children at the Fulford Street Nursery in London. French, an experienced administrator, led CARE during its first 10 years of extraordinary growth. His businesslike approach to charity—using sophisticated sales, marketing and distribution methods—prompted the *New York Herald-Tribune* to call him a "hard-nosed do-gooder." *(CARE photo)*

"What also touched me, maybe not until later, maybe not when I was a child, was that the people that sent us the packages had been our enemies just a few years earlier, and the war was a terrible thing, and they had every right to feel hostile towards us, and they didn't. They helped us, and that was a very valuable gift as well."

— TRUDY MCVICKER, who received CARE Packages in 1946 in Bavaria when she was a refugee.

LEFT: Children in a bombed-out building in Italy take stock of their gift from America.

(CARE photo)

The Lord Mayor and town council of Hanford, England, gather to accept a shipment of packages sent by a civic group in Hanford, California. Gifts like this became common, and often challenged the resourcefulness of CARE mission chiefs, who had to make sure the donors' instructions were met. A schoolteacher in Milwaukee asked that a package be sent to a teacher with two cats in France. A boy in New Jersey sent a package to the dirtiest boy in Berlin. And one donor even asked that his package go to a tall brunette with dark eyes and sultry lips. *(CARE photo)*

"When the day-and-night shooting and bombing were over, when we found out that our doors were not locked any longer, that we could go home, I experienced very slowly the worst hours. I had no strength to hold to anything, to stand, to put one foot in front of the other one. I had no shoes, no home, no food, no friends, no relatives. No one looked at me or called my name. And then a miracle happened. A CARE Package came for me. With a blanket, with some food, some warm socks. I never found out who paid for it. It was a beginning."

— MARGOT MEURTENS,
who survived the Holocaust and received a CARE Package at a U.S. Army hospital in Germany.

LEFT: CARE Package recipients, like this girl in Germany, often wrote thank-you notes to senders in America. In many cases, the correspondence grew into friendships that lasted for lifetimes. *(CARE photo)*

BELOW AND RIGHT: A thank-you from the director of a Korean orphanage to Lucy Hotinger's second-grade class in Columbia, South Carolina.

SO SAENG WON ORPHANAGE
Unchondong Chongju
Chungchong Pukto, Korea
June 14, 1957

Mrs. Lucy S Hotinger &
2nd grade Class
So Kilbourne School
1327 S Bettline Blvd
Columbia S. C.

Dear Friends:

A CARE Package of Basic Food you have sent to Korea for the un-fortunates through CARE Korea Agnecy have received by this orphanage with gratitude. Those package materilly kept the health of the children of this orphanage and encouraged them in their austere way of life. It also encouraged me beyond words to adequately express it. We shall never forget the kindness you have shown usthrough the packages.

On behalf of the 56 children of this orphanage, I want to express my sincere gratitude to you again and wish you a great deal of happiness and blessings in the Lord Jeses Christ.

Yours very truly,

Lee Man Chung

Lee Man Chung
Superintendent

LEE MAN CHUNG
SO SAENG WON ORPHANAGE
Unchondong, Chongju
Chungchong Pukto, Korea

VIA AIR MAIL

Mrs Lucy S Hotinger &
2nd Grade Class
So Kilbourne School
1327 S Bettline Blvd
Columbia S. C.
U.S.A.

RIGHT: Every donor received a receipt signed by the beneficiary. In some cases, the signature was the first sign that a friend or a relative had survived the war. The punch card system, developed for CARE by Remington-Rand, put CARE at the technological cutting edge in 1947 and helped it cope with its rapid growth.

LEFT: As Europe recovered, CARE began to diversify geographically and in the content of packages. This 1952 photo shows Japanese children with a CARE Children's Literature Package. By the early 1950s, CARE was working in Asia, Latin America and the Middle East, in addition to Europe. (CARE photo)

RIGHT: Vietnamese children carry CARE Packages at a refugee settlement in 1965. All through the late 1950s and early 1960s, the CARE Package became a smaller part of CARE's operations, as self-help projects and donated U.S. commodities grew in prominence. In 1966, the famous package was "retired," though it has been revived several times, most recently in Bosnia. (CARE photo)

In Hong Kong, CARE Packages eased the struggle of Chinese refugees fleeing the upheaval of the 1949 revolution. *(CARE photo)*

In the
SPOTLIGHT

**Charlton Heston visits
with children in Somalia
during the 1992 famine
and civil war.** *(CARE
photo by Carolyn Snyder)*

On a rough Atlantic crossing in the winter of 1948, CARE executive director Paul French was resting in his second-class cabin, a bit seasick and thoroughly exhausted from a monthlong tour of CARE operations in Europe. A steward woke him from a deep sleep and informed him that the gentleman in charge of the CARE organization wished to buy him a drink in the private club bar. "But I'm the gentleman in charge of CARE," he told the steward, who shrugged and led him to an elegant room with oak walls, Tiffany lamps and a faint smell of cigar smoke. There, behind a martini and a mischievous smile, was the unmistakable countenance of Douglas Fairbanks Jr.

Though he wasn't quite running the organization, Fairbanks, more than anyone else, had pushed CARE into the public spotlight, beginning a long history of celebrity support that continues to this day. Since CARE's founding, the dashing film star had been urging Americans—and his friends in Hollywood—to support the new agency. Fairbanks founded the "Share Through CARE" committee, handed out packages in Rome, helped CARE get its own ABC radio show and, most important, gave CARE's publicity department access to dozens of Hollywood's top stars. He even led a campaign to send 1,000 CARE Packages to England as a wedding present to Princess Elizabeth in

1947—and delivered them himself.

Since then, hundreds of the famous and near-famous—from presidents and painters to athletes and actors—have helped CARE tell its story to the world. Even before Fairbanks's efforts, President Harry S. Truman endorsed CARE at a White House ceremony that was broadcast on radio and newsreel; he even purchased 100 CARE Packages himself and had them sent to 10 heads of state in Europe.

On the other side of the Atlantic, many famous Europeans received packages from admirers and also helped CARE promote its mission. Finnish composer Jan Sibelius accepted a shipment of four 29-pound parcels during a severe food shortage in Helsinki. A CARE press release reported that "his only disappointment was the absence of a cigar." And the Soprano Elizabeth Schwarzkopf, who practiced her arias in a bomb shelter during the war, was paid in CARE Packages for singing to American GIs in an Austrian hospital. Other CARE Package recipients weren't yet famous but would be someday. German chancellor Helmut Kohl, for example, has fond memories of CARE Packages he received as a young boy, as does actress Elke Sommer.

Every U.S. president since Truman has endorsed the organization. President John F. Kennedy, who called on CARE to train the first Peace Corps volunteers in

1961, wrote in a 1962 letter to CARE officials: "I know the trust and esteem the American people have gained in country after country because of the aid CARE provides in their name. . . Every CARE Package is a personal contribution to the world peace our nation seeks. It expresses America's concern and friendship in a language all peoples can understand."

Today, CARE continues to receive support from prominent Americans. Whoopi Goldberg, the Academy Award winning actress, appeared in CARE's 50th Anniversary public-service announcements. And former presidents Jimmy Carter, Gerald Ford and George Bush took part in CARE's World Leadership Tribute in 1995, urging Americans to remain engaged in international affairs.

Douglas Fairbanks Jr., an early CARE advocate, delivers a CARE Package to a family living in a cave in Rome. *(CARE photo)*

R.WT.29¼ lRS CU. FT. 1'4"

U.S.A.

21-3

ABOVE: Fairbanks not only promoted CARE himself but also convinced many of his Hollywood friends to help out. Here, he looks through a package with Joan Fontaine 1947. (*CARE photo*)

LEFT: Nearly 50 years after he first told the world about CARE, Douglas Fairbanks Jr. is honored at CARE's 50th Anniversary World Leadership Tribute in 1995. With him is Guy Arledge, CARE's Director of Communications.

(*CARE photo*)

Maurice Chevalier was one of many European stars who helped promote CARE Packages. *(CARE photo)*

ABOVE: The Von Trapp Family Singers, who inspired *The Sound of Music*, ordered 120 CARE Packages for Austria in 1946, using $1,200 they had raised from the sale of souvenir programs. Presenting the check is Johannes Von Trapp; accepting it is the Reverand James H. Doyle of Boston. *(CARE photo)*

ABOVE: Finnish composer Jan Sibelius, left, receives a CARE Package at his home in Bilinki, Finland. At right is CARE's mission chief, Reider K. Asper. The infamous also received packages on occasion: When Hitler's interpreter was arrested, they found a large number of CARE Packages in his home. *(CARE photo)*

ABOVE: Jean Simmons receives a CARE Package sent by two Standard Oil Company executives who admired her portrayal of Ophelia in Laurence Olivier's production of *Hamlet*. At far left is actor Stanley Holloway; presenting the package is CARE's mission chief in London, Einer Olsen. *(CARE photo)*

Actor James Mason and his wife send a CARE Package to her sister in Surrey, England, in 1948. Also pictured are CARE executive director Paul Comly French (receiving check) and British consul general Sir Francis Evans. *(CARE photo)*

Marlene Dietrich visits a boy in Israel in the early 1950s. *(CARE photo)*

LEFT: Ingrid Bergman in 1949. The film legend supported CARE throughout the 1950s, in part by recording several public-service radio ads. (*CARE photo*)

RIGHT: Danny Kaye with the recipient of the first CARE Package to Britain in 1946. Kaye was one of the first of many stars to distribute CARE Packages while working or traveling in Europe. (*CARE photo*)

ABOVE: Paulette Goddard visits children at the Hague Street School in the East End of London. (*CARE photo*)

ABOVE: Mynra Loy presents a package to Maria Sacripanti and her brother, Giuseppe, the children of an Italian actor who was wounded and disabled during the war. The photograph taken in Rome, is from 1948. (*CARE photo*)

ABOVE: The Duke of Windsor presents a check to a CARE official in 1947. Other European royalty were also involved with CARE. Queen Wilhelmina of the Netherlands received hundreds of packages from American admirers and distributed them to the needy. *(CARE photo)*

ABOVE: Joe Louis (right), the heavyweight champion and boxing legend, was one of the first individuals to purchase a CARE Package in 1946. Note on the sign that the price had dropped from $15 to $10, a tactic used to combat slow initial sales. *(CARE photo)*

RIGHT: Gregory Peck distributes CARE Packages in Greece in the early 1950s. *(CARE photo)*

ABOVE: Yul Brynner presents a CARE school kit at the National Girls' Orphanage in Rhodes, Greece, in the 1950s. *(CARE photo)*

ABOVE: Anthony Quinn, in Greece to film *Zorba the Greek*, visits with children involved in a CARE nutrition project in 1962. *(CARE photo)*

ABOVE: Joseph Cotten takes time out from filming *The Third Man* to distribute CARE Packages in Vienna in 1948. Ironically, the classic film centers on a fraudulent charity (masterminded by Orson Welles) and its violent black-market dealings in postwar Austria. *(CARE photo)*

BELOW: Lauren Bacall taking note of a CARE Package, and an improbable hat, in the early 1950s. *(CARE photo)*

ABOVE: Janet Leigh and her daughter, Jamie Lee Curtis, led a CARE Mother's Day fund-raising effort in the 1980s, drawing attention to the need for mother-child health programs in developing nations. *(CARE photo)*

ABOVE: Marlon Brando and Karl Malden, fresh from their triumph in *A Streetcar Named Desire,* hosted a CARE benefit in the 1950s. *(CARE photo)*

ABOVE: Four decades later, during his own Broadway success in the Tennessee Williams classic, Alec Baldwin hosted another *A Streetcar Named Desire* benefit for CARE in 1993. *(CARE photo)*

ABOVE: Bob Geldof, the British rock star, visits refugee children at a CARE health center in Mozambique in the late 1980s. Geldof helped focus concern on the famine in Africa in 1985, raising tens of millions of dollars and introducing a new generation to the need for international aid programs. CARE was one of many agencies to receive funding from Geldof's efforts and the "We Are the World" campaign. *(CARE photo by Robin Needham)*

LEFT: Actress Whoopi Goldberg has been the organization's most visible supporter in the 1990s. She appeared in CARE's 50th Anniversary public-service advertising campaign, which was aired on hundreds of television stations nationwide. *(CARE photo)*

ABOVE: Dikembe Mutombo, the star center for the Denver Nuggets and a native of Zaire, visits CARE projects in Kenya in 1993. In the 1990s, the National Basketball Association has been a key supporter of CARE, hosting benefit games and airing public-service announcements during televised games. The National Football League had a similar program with CARE in the 1980s, while baseball stars such as Yogi Berra supported CARE in the 1950s and '60s. *(CARE photo by Don Pohl)*

ABOVE: Ronald Reagan sifts through a CARE Package in 1947. As president, he honored CARE with a Presidential World Without Hunger Award, while Nancy Reagan chaired CARE's 40th Anniversary Celebration. After leaving office, he urged Americans to send CARE Packages to Russia after the end of the Cold War and recalled how sending packages to Germany after World War II helped form bonds of friendship. *"Only those who received them will ever fully appreciate what a CARE Package meant—and continues to mean: comfort in the present and hope for the future."—1986* (CARE photo)

ABOVE: General Dwight D. Eisenhower appears with CARE executive director General William N. Haskell in 1946. As president, Eisenhower would sign legislation that allowed CARE to use vast amounts of American surplus food to fight hunger overseas. And like President Truman before him—and every president since—he publicly endorsed CARE's work to the American people. *"Everywhere, CARE is strengthening the belief and confidence in democratic processes."—1954* (CARE photo)

ABOVE: Vice President Lyndon Johnson and his wife, Lady Bird, serve milk to children at a CARE nutrition center in Cyprus in 1962. *"The fight against povery cannot end at home. . . .The food, self-help and medical supplies and services CARE provides are basic weapons in the fight against hunger, poverty and disease."—1964.* (CARE photo)

ABOVE: Vice President Richard Nixon walks through a flag-waving crowd in Bogatá, Colombia, on his way to visit a CARE health center in 1958. *"CARE is a vital forum for bringing to the attention of our people the needs of the world's less fortunate and rallying them to their assistance."—1971* (CARE photo)

ABOVE: Vice President George Bush and his wife, Barbara, meet CARE president Philip Johnston in Sudan in 1982. Twelve years later, CARE honored President Bush with its International Humanitarian Award for his decision to use U.S. troops to end the famine in Somalia. *"Since 1946 CARE has been the conscience of our country."—1994* (CARE photo)

ABOVE: Former president Jimmy Carter and his wife, Rosalynn, visit with CARE staff in southern Sudan in 1995. As first lady, Mrs. Carter urged Americans to respond to the refugee crisis in Cambodia in 1979, while Carter has been a forceful advocate for humanitarian and human-rights issues through the Carter Center. *"When the Carter Center goes to any place in the most remote areas where the needs are greatest, CARE is always there."—1995* (CARE photo)

ABOVE: Indian prime minister Jawaharlal Nehru inspects CARE tools and a plow donated by Americans for Indian farmers in 1952. *(CARE photo)*

LEFT: President Anwar Sadat of Egypt visits a CARE solar-energy project in 1980. *(CARE photo)*

RIGHT: Pope Paul VI presents CARE executive director Frank Goffio with a medal in 1965 during a ceremony marking the end of CARE's operations in Italy, the last nation in Western Europe where CARE worked. *(CARE photo)*

ABOVE: In 1992, CARE honored General Colin Powell for the assistance the U.S. military provided to CARE during the Kurdish refugee crisis following the Gulf War. Presenting the award is Marilyn Quayle, wife of the Vice President Dan Quayle. *(CARE photo)*

Partners AT HOME

In 1948, members of Cub Scout Pack 232 from Bethesda, Maryland, present Secretary of State George Marshall with their "Junior Marshall Plan." The Scouts aimed to provide five youngsters in Europe with CARE Packages for one year by hosting a benefit movie at a local theater.

(CARE photo)

When five-year-old Evan Towt's parents told him that he couldn't send sandwiches to the hungry in Somalia, he decided to raise money for CARE instead. The kindergartner from Gillette, New Jersey, made Christmas ornaments and sold them at a local grocery store. He raised a total of $53.06. His mother, Irene Towt, sent the proceeds to CARE along with an explanation: "Evan is truly the one with the initiative—we did not push him into it. He kept saying, 'Mom, when are we going to do something for the Somalis?'"

This individual initiative is the essence of CARE. It has been at work since the organization's founding, when labor unions, religious groups, women's clubs, Boy Scouts, and Americans from all walks of life began sending CARE Packages to Europe. Many of them first heard about CARE through the considerable efforts of the Advertising Council, which provided CARE with enormous amounts of free public-service advertising from 1947 until the late 1950s.

Corporations began supporting CARE by sending packages to employees in their European offices. Others donated food and other goods that would go into CARE Packages, although most of the items were purchased by CARE. Today, more than 250 major corporations serve on CARE's Corporate Council, founded by Peter Drucker and now led by William T. Esrey, chairman and CEO of Sprint. CARE's 50th Anniversary sponsors are Delta Air Lines, Masco Home Furnishings, Microsoft Corporation, Sprint, Starbucks Coffee Company, Westin Hotels & Resorts, and the Interpublic Group of Companies (parent company of the advertising agencies McCann-Erickson, Ammirati & Puris/Lintas, Lowe).

Volunteers have helped CARE throughout the years, serving as board members, raising money, increasing awareness and working at everything from serving as health workers overseas to chairing the Corporate Council. Today, CARE's volunteer network is organized through the CARE Foundation, which also seeks major gifts for the organization.

CARE has also received significant funding from the U.S. government, other governments and major institutional donors such as the United Nations and the World Bank; much of the funding has been in the form of donated food commodities. In addition, host governments often share project costs. And finally, the project participants—the people CARE ultimately serves—contribute their own energy and talents. CARE's work, by any definition, is a partnership between people who want to help the world and those who are eager for the opportunity to build better lives for their families.

Over the years, some 35 million Americans have supported CARE, along with many thousands of Canadians, Europeans, Japanese and Australians, through CARE International. All this support, over 50 years, has enabled CARE to reach some one billion people in 125 countries with $7.5 billion in aid. Every day, individuals and organizations in America and around the world continue this tradition and make the decision to make a difference in the world. This spirit of generosity is at the heart of CARE and everything it does.

A CARE poster, created by the Advertising Council, circa 1950.

Help
Freedom!

CARE
U.S.A.

N2 1102
CA 001

Send
Another Care Package
Overseas Today!

LEFT: Cartoon from 1950. Early in its history, CARE was often promoted as a way to support freedom and fight Communism and extreme nationalism.

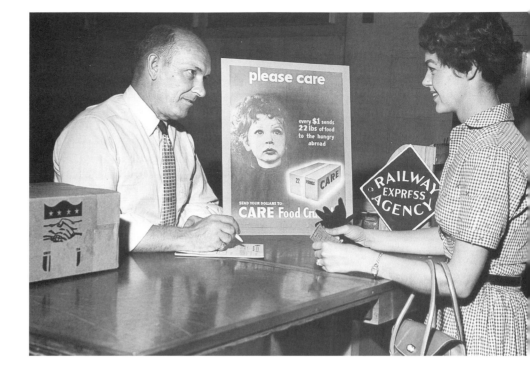

LEFT: With messages like this one from 1956, the Advertising Council helped make CARE a household name. The council, then and now, is the advertising industry's way of promoting worthy causes and bringing attention to social problems. For 10 years beginning in 1947, CARE received tens of millions of dollars in free public-service advertising in newspapers, magazines, radio, television and billboards. Today, Ruth A. Wooden, president of the Ad Council, serves on CARE's Board of Directors. *(CARE photo)*

ABOVE: A CARE Package is purchased in 1956 at a Philadelphia Railway Express office. Donors could purchase packages at department stores, regional CARE offices or through countless civic groups.

ABOVE: Workers at CARE's packing plant in Philadelphia (left) take stock of seeds donated by the Burpee Seed Company, which continues to support CARE today. The seeds were included in special gardening packages that helped people, like these Berliners (right), grow their own food and return to self-sufficiency. (Note the Brandenburg Gate in the background). *(CARE photos)*

ABOVE: Toni, the maker of the famous home permanent kit, combined its Toni Twins campaign with a CARE Package promotion. These Toni Twins, armed with CARE Packages, are about to embark on a European tour in 1948. *(CARE photo)*

LEFT: An early corporate supporter was Lever Brothers, which launched a campaign in 1949 to donate a bar of soap to CARE for every two Swan soap wrappers turned in by American consumers. Bob Hope, shown here receiving a wrapper and a kiss, was the spokesman for the campaign, which he plugged on his popular radio show. Eventually more than 1.3 million bars of soap were shipped to needy families overseas. *(CARE photo)*

RIGHT: Condé Nast Publishing arranged for its American employees to send CARE Packages to their counterparts in Europe after the war. This typist at *British Vogue* inspects her CARE Package in 1947. *(CARE photo)*

ABOVE: In the late 1940s, CARE had its own radio show on ABC, called *We CARE*. Note a young Tony Randall checking his script in the background. In the 1950s, CARE tried television, airing a variety program called the *CARE TV Theatre*. Despite appearances by Victor Borge and Cab Calloway, the program failed to take the new medium by storm. *(CARE photo)*

BELOW: The Starbucks Coffee Company, which is committed to helping the developing countries where its coffee is grown, is CARE's largest corporate supporter today. Here, Starbucks vice president Dave Olsen examines the fruits of a CARE agroforestry project his company is sponsoring in Guatemala. *(CARE photo)*

In Ethiopia, an arid land of dramatic landscapes, the Starbucks Coffee Company's support is helping farmers improve agricultural methods and irrigation while preserving the country's natural forests. *(CARE photo by Scott Faiia)*

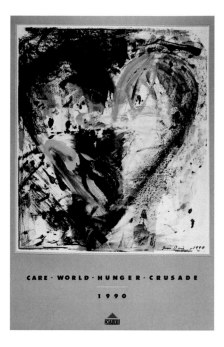

CARE · WORLD · HUNGER · CRUSADE
1990

© Roy Lichtenstein CARE Poster 1993 Painted & printed paper on board 39 3/4" x 27 1/8"

CARE World Hunger Crusade 1993

WORLD HUNGER CRUSADE 1994

Since 1990, renowned American artists have been creating posters to promote the World Hunger Crusade, CARE's annual campaign to educate Americans about global hunger. Shown here is the work of Jim Dine (top, 1990), Roy Lichtenstein (left, 1993) and Edward Gorey (above, 1994).

RIGHT: Individuals give to CARE for a variety of reasons. Sometimes, as with this water system in rural Haiti, their contributions are in memory of departed loved ones. *(CARE photo)*

ABOVE: Children in Peru display a holiday greeting from Westin Hotels & Resorts, a sponsor of CARE's 50th Anniversary and of various CARE projects worldwide. *(CARE photo by Kim Johnston)*

RIGHT: Adele Hall, a devoted CARE supporter and the wife of Donald Hall, chairman of Hallmark Inc., visits a CARE project she supports in Ecuador. Thanks to the contributions of Mrs. Hall and other donors, the project is providing safe drinking water and improved health services to an impoverished region. *(CARE photo)*

LEFT: In 1995, three American presidents helped CARE celebrate its 50th Anniversary at the organization's World Leadership Tribute. The event honored every American president since Harry S. Truman for their contribution to global understanding and progress. The event was sponsored by Sprint and held in seven cities linked by a live video broadcast. Pictured here in New York (top left) is Sprint chairman and CEO William T. Esrey, who hosted the evening, along with television journalist Bill Kurtis. At the tribute in Atlanta (bottom), former president Jimmy Carter was honored and is pictured here with (left) Peter D. Bell, CARE's president, and James C. Kennedy, chairman and CEO of Cox Enterprises, Inc. *(CARE photo)*

BELOW: Children today are still showing they care. This boy was one of hundreds at The Children's School in Atlanta who packed CARE Packages of school supplies for children in Bosnia in 1995. *(CARE photo by Suzy Hopper)*

TOP: Perhaps the most famous picture associated with CARE was taken by *National Geographic* photographer William Albert Allard in 1982. It shows a Peruvian shepherd boy, Eduardo Condor Ramos, moments after a taxi struck and killed six of his sheep. Hundreds of readers, moved by the tragedy, sent contributions to the magazine, which turned to CARE for help in spending the funds wisely. ABOVE: Weeks later, CARE assistant executive director Ronald Burkard delivered six new animals to Eduardo, who, through his tears, said, "God will pay you." There was even enough money for CARE to build a school in the tiny mountain village of Ichu. CARE staff in Peru recently tracked down Eduardo, now a mechanic in Lima, who remembered the day fondly.
Top: *(Photo © 1982 by William Albert Allard)*
Bottom: *(CARE photo by Niels Lindquist)*

Triumph OVER TRAGEDY

Ethiopians gather in a displaced person's camp during the 1985 famine.
(CARE photo by Rudolph von Bernuth)

*"I've been there with the refugees in almost every part of the world....
It is a great honor to say to you that there's no place in the world
where I have visited tragedy that CARE hasn't been there first."*

— ABC NEWS ANCHOR PETER JENNINGS,
CARE Corporate Council reception, 1994

Floods. Hurricanes. Earth-quakes. Famine. War. Regard-less of the form disaster takes, the results are all too similar: suffering and deprivation for innocent people, many of them the poorest, the youngest or the oldest in their respective communities.

From the Berlin blockade of 1948-49 to the African famine of 1984-85, from the 1956 Hungarian refugee crisis to ethnic conflicts in Rwanda and Bosnia today, CARE has been at the forefront of efforts to ease the suffering and help people regain control of their lives.

CARE was born as a relief agency, designed to send help to people recovering from World War II. But within a few years, CARE began employing the same basic tool— the CARE Package—in response to other emergencies in Europe, including the Berlin blockade, a major drought in Yugoslavia and severe flooding in Holland.

The strife surrounding the creation of Israel and the outbreak of war in Korea took CARE's relief operations outside Europe in 1949-50. In the years that followed, CARE continued to send emergency-package shipments to disaster survivors around the world. But in the late 1960s, two

famines—the first in Bihar, India, and the second in Nigeria/Biafra— changed the nature of CARE's relief work. Instead of just sending packages, CARE began managing the delivery of massive amounts of food commodities to stricken people. In addition, CARE began working with the United Nations to set up and maintain camps for refugees and displaced persons.

In the 1970s and '80s, similar famines ensued, often a deadly mix of drought and civil war, with many of the conflicts rooted in the Cold War. In Angola, Mozambique, Somalia, Sudan, Ethiopia, Cambodia and elsewhere, protracted struggles between governments backed by one superpower and guerrilla armies backed by another left economies and food production in shambles. When droughts occurred—and often even when they didn't—the effects were devastating.

The worst famine of the century hit in 1984-85 throughout east and north Africa. Television footage, especially from Ethiopia, shocked the world and prompted an unprecedented international response. More than one million people perished in the famine, but many millions more were saved. CARE alone provided food for

some six million people throughout the region.

After the famine, CARE stayed on in many countries and helped survivors begin to rebuild their lives by providing seeds and tools, new livestock and agricultural training and by helping villages build more reliable water supplies. CARE has also helped develop early-warning systems in Ethiopia designed to spot famine conditions and take preventive action. This progression from relief to rehabilitation to development is a cornerstone of CARE's programming philosophy.

The end of the Cold War led many relief officials to hope for a reduction in humanitarian emergencies. And in many countries, such as El Salvador, Angola and Cambodia, the absence of superpower tensions helped begin a slow but steady peace process. But in many other lands, the "new world order" has resulted instead in massive disorder. Ethnic and tribal tensions kept in check during the Cold War have exploded into horrific violence in Somalia, Rwanda, Bosnia, Armenia, Azerbaijan and elsewhere.

In this dangerous environment, mounting an effective response is fraught with difficulties. Huge quantities of food and supplies must be moved through remote and often treacherous regions. Systems for storing, distributing and accounting for the food must be created rapidly. Added to traditional logistical problems such as finding enough trucks, fuel and local staff are new obstacles: land mines, sniper fire and combatants who will halt relief supplies in order to starve the women and children of their enemies.

All the while, relief workers must face the sobering fact that they themselves may be targeted if they are perceived to be "on the wrong side." The job, never an easy one, has become a physical and emotional ordeal that tests the limits of human endurance. In the Somalia crisis of 1992, CARE workers, many sick with malaria, worked 16-hour days in 100-degree heat, surrounded by gunfire and the specter of starving children. Yet none asked for transfers, and when their tour of duty was over, many refused to leave.

For 50 years, this has been the pattern, and hope has been the product. Hope not only to survive but to grow and to flourish, even in the wake of humankind's greatest tragedies.

When Soviet troops blockaded Berlin in 1948, the first major crisis of the Cold War ensued. The United States responded with the now-famous airlift, which included 250,000 CARE Packages, 60 percent of all relief sent to the city. When the blockade was lifted in May 1949, CARE trucks, the first vehicles to enter the city, were greeted with a roaring welcome by crowds of Berliners. *(CARE Photo)*

Newspaper headlines report how CARE became caught up in the rise of Cold War tensions during the late 1940s. As Communist governments swept into power in Eastern Europe, CARE's operations faced increasing harassment by authorities who regarded American agencies as tools of capitalist propaganda. In Romania, CARE's mission chief was jailed three times before fleeing the country. In Czechoslovakia, authorities tapped CARE's phone lines and shadowed its employees through the streets of Prague. CARE's mission chief in Warsaw, a devout Quaker, protested the government's obstruction of CARE food shipments by eating only what the average Pole ate, and later died of complications brought on by malnutrition. Bulgarian citizens working for CARE were threatened and forced to quit. By 1950, CARE was forced to close all of its missions in Eastern Europe, except for those in Yugoslavia. But according to one staffer, CARE continued to send aid beyond the Iron Curtain, using grandmotherly German volunteers to carry CARE Packages wrapped as gifts past border guards into East Berlin in the 1950s. Back in the States, the media portrayed CARE as a force for goodwill that transcended politics.

When Soviet troops invaded Hungary in 1956, thousands of refugees fleeing into Austria received help from CARE.

(CARE photo)

ABOVE: America's wars in Korea and Vietnam prompted millions of Americans to send relief through CARE. In 1963, Pat Reardon, a doctor with CARE's MEDICO division, treats a young victim of the growing conflict in Vietnam. *(CARE photo)*

LEFT: In 1950, Yugoslavia, defying the Soviet Union, called on CARE's help during a devastating drought. Using U.S.-government surplus food to supplement CARE Packages, the organization mounted what at the time was the largest private relief operation in history, sending food to some two million people. *(CARE photo)*

ABOVE AND RIGHT:
Cambodian refugee children in
South Vietnam in 1975, just
before the fall of Saigon.
(CARE photos by Kerry Heubeck)

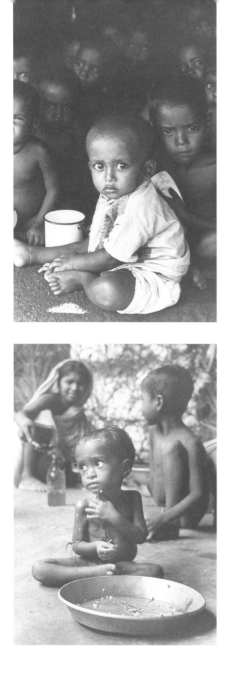

In 1971, dual calamities struck the Indian subcontinent, as a civil war and a deadly cyclone devastated East Pakistan (soon to become Bangladesh), sending refugees, like these boys (top), streaming into India. The plight of the new nation of Bangladesh, meanwhile, captured the world's attention, including Beatle George Harrison, who gathered many rock stars and produced a best-selling album. This photo (above) graced the cover, and part of the proceeds went to **CARE.** *(CARE photos)*

ABOVE AND RIGHT: CARE provided assistance to hundreds of thousands of Bangladeshis in 1988, when floodwaters covered three-quarters of the nation. The country's high population density and severe poverty have made cyclones and flooding particularly deadly over the years. *(CARE photos by Rudolph von Bernuth, above, and Guy Stallworthy, right)*

CARE provided aid to refugees from Cambodian political and social upheaval in the 1970s and '80s. TOP: A refugee camp in Thailand in 1984. *(CARE Photo by Rudolph von Bernuth)* **ABOVE LEFT: A young refugee gets a nutritious meal in 1984.** *(CARE Photo by Rudolph von Bernuth)* **ABOVE RIGHT: In 1979, a young girl is among thousands of Cambodians who have fled the brutality of the Pol Pot regime and its "killing fields."** *(CARE photo)*

ABOVE: A boy in Ethiopia during the famine of 1984-85. CARE provided food and other necessities for six million people during the worst famine of the century, which killed an estimated one million people. CARE worked in many of the hardest-hit countries, including Ethiopia, Sudan, Somalia, Chad, Mali, Niger, Kenya and Mauritania. The American public responded in unprecedented numbers during the crisis, almost doubling their donations to CARE in a single year. *(CARE photo by Rudolph von Bernuth)*

TOP RIGHT: Life for millions of Africans—like this child in Sudan—centered around stark refugee camps, where CARE, the United Nations and other agencies provided food, shelter and health care. *(CARE photo by H. Shaw McCutcheon)*

BOTTOM RIGHT: In Sudan, the arrival of food brings renewed hope. *(CARE photo by H. Shaw McCutcheon)*

ABOVE: In 1981, CARE Packages returned to the streets of Europe for the first time in 25 years during a severe food shortage in Poland, where the Solidarity movement was challenging the Communist government.

ABOVE: In 1988, CARE sent aid to the Soviet Union for the first time ever when a devastating earthquake killed 23,000 people in Armenia. This five-year-old girl named Anna lost everything but a tricycle and a few Christmas ornaments. When the Cold War ended over the next two years, CARE USA and CARE International members in Europe began numerous initiatives in the former Soviet bloc. CARE Germany, reminding Germans of the packages they received after World War II, sent 600,000 food parcels to Russia in 1990-91. *(CARE photo by Rudolph von Bernuth)*

RIGHT: A CARE worker distributes supplies to Kurdish refugees in the rugged mountains along the border between Turkey and Iraq in the wake of the 1991 Persian Gulf War. CARE provided food, water, tents and blankets for some one million Kurds, Shiites and ethnic Turks who fled Iraq during and after the conflict. *(CARE photo by Sandra Laumark)*

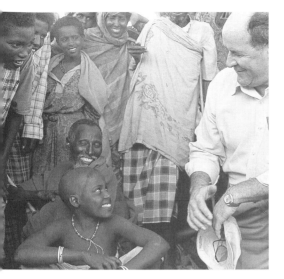

LEFT: CARE president Dr. Philip Johnston greets a child in Somalia. Johnston (now president of the CARE Foundation) took a leave of absence from CARE to serve as United Nations coordinator for humanitarian assistance in Somalia in 1992-93 and advocated forcefully for an international effort to address the crisis. CARE provided seeds, tools and agricultural support that helped Somali farmers recover from the civil war. *(CARE photo by Fiona McDougal)*

ABOVE: The crisis in Somalia presented CARE with what was perhaps its most difficult, and dangerous, relief operation ever. Until the arrival of U.S. troops in December 1992, CARE food shipments were constantly hijacked by rival clans, and several Somali drivers were killed and wounded. The Somali businessmen who rented vehicles to relief agencies required that armed guards ride along; usually that meant a few teenagers with AK-47s, as seen here (note the grenade launcher on the roof). This situation was even less comforting for relief workers when they learned that the guards were there to protect the vehicle, not the occupants. *(CARE photo by Zed Nelson)*

TOP LEFT: Children in Mozambique, where CARE is helping a nation now recovering from a long period of civil strife. *(CARE photo by Sarah Eranston)*

TOP RIGHT: During the worst refugee crisis in recent memory, a CARE food truck inches its way through teeming crowds of Rwandan refugees near Goma, Zaire. More than two million Rwandans fled to neighboring countries during a brutal outbreak of ethnic and political violence in 1994.
(CARE photo by David Morris)

ABOVE: In Kibungo, Rwanda, a woman recovers in a makeshift hospital. *(Photo © 1994 by Yael Swedlow)*

A Refugee's Story

For one Rwandan refugee, a CARE station in Tanzania has been a sanctuary from the horrors of war. Munyantwali Valens, 39, fled from his home with his wife and six children as Rwanda dissolved into violence in April 1994. He told this story to relief workers after arriving at CARE's Benaco Refugee Camp:

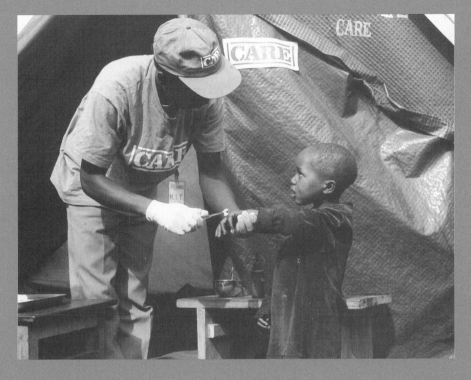

"We walked for one and a half weeks. It was the season of heavy rains, and because we had no shelter my two daughters contracted pneumonia and died. On 4 May, we arrived at a hill in the Ngara region of Tanzania that would become Benaco Camp. We had run out of food a few days before and were sure that we would die of starvation. Most of the other refugees were in the same condition—no food, little water, no shelter, sitting in the rain. At this time, our two youngest sons died. Now only our two oldest sons were left, and they were so thin and sick.

A CARE health worker administers first aid to a young refugee. Children were not spared the horror of mass executions and accounted for many of the 500,000 victims of genocide. *(CARE photo by Alex Tibbetts)*

"Finally we heard that help was coming. There were many organizations, but we were glad to learn that one of them was familiar to us—CARE. CARE worked in Rwanda before the war, building water systems and doing forestry. Very soon after their arrival, CARE began to dig latrines and to help us keep them clean and maintained. CARE also distributes food and other items like cookware, fuel wood, clothes and soap to our commune. Myself and my family have lost much in the last months. We are like all of the other people here. But we are thankful to be alive. And when our two sons awake in the morning and they are eager to fetch water or firewood, we can still feel some happiness and hope. For these things we must thank CARE."

In Search OF SOLUTIONS

Women crush grain in Niger, where CARE agricultural programs are helping farmers make more productive use of their land. *(CARE photo by Rudolph von Bernuth)*

Before World War II, few Americans beyond religious missionaries gave much thought to the plight of the poor overseas. The lands and peoples of Africa, Asia and even Latin America were seen mostly through the prism of colonialism, jungle movies and dime-store novels. But in the last 50 years, the creation of the United Nations, the end of colonial empires and the advance of technology and communications have brought the developing world, and its problems, into America's field of view. The response of many Americans—as well as Europeans, Canadians and citizens of developing nations themselves—has been a search for solutions to global poverty on a scale unmatched in human history.

For CARE, the search began in 1948, when seeds and tools were included in CARE Packages, providing recipients with the means to improve their lives. In the following year, CARE began work in the Philippines and India, bringing its aid for the first time to the poor in developing nations.

In the 1950s and '60s, the word *self-help* permeated almost everything CARE did. It meant providing packages with everything from shoemaker's kits to dental equipment. It meant giving Korean war widows sewing machines so they could earn a living. It meant developing a better plow so farmers in India could grow more food.

In the late 1960s and into the '70s, CARE moved beyond simply giving useful items to the poor and began initiating projects that improved village life. Schools, wells and latrines were built, with local people doing much of the work themselves. Many of the schools, throughout Latin America in particular, are still standing.

At the same time, CARE began addressing health concerns, first in 1962 by affiliating with MEDICO, an agency that sent doctors overseas, and later by training health workers, promoting immunizations and providing food for mothers and children. In the years that followed, these low-cost health-care initiatives, championed by CARE and other development agencies, led to startling reductions in infant mortality, saving the lives of an estimated three million children annually.

In the 1980s and '90s, CARE broadened its focus to include a host of new concerns—natural-resource management, population and family planning, AIDS awareness, income generation and girls' education, while continuing a strong commitment to health, water and nutrition programs.

Throughout CARE's history, donated food commodities have been an important resource in combating hunger and poverty. The Agricultural Act of 1949 allowed CARE and other organizations to ship large quantities of American surplus food to people in need. In 1954, Public Law 480 made even more surplus food available at a time when CARE's operations in Europe were ending. Within a few years, Food for Peace, as the program came to be known, became CARE's single largest resource. Over the years, CARE has used hundreds of million of dollars' worth of donated commodities to provide school lunches, to supplement the diets of pregnant and nursing mothers, as payment for "Food for Work" projects that built roads and schools, and to help refugees and disaster victims. Today, CARE also sells commodities on local markets and uses the proceeds to fund development programs.

A great challenge of development programs today is sustaining social or economic progress after a project ends—and in ways that don't jeopardize natural resources for future generations. It is a complex task, fraught with the potential to do more harm than good if great sensitivity isn't paid to the needs, abilities and cultural context of the people being assisted.

Helping people, in short, is far more difficult than most people would imagine. Despite the complexity, the past 50 years have shown that meaningful assistance can be provided—efficiently and sustainably. But it requires a true partnership and a commitment not only to help people in need, but to believe in their ability to solve their own problems.

A Hong Kong fisherman inspects a net from a CARE fisherman's kit in 1957. *(CARE photo)*

ABOVE: Dr. Albert Schweitzer, the Nobel laureate who founded a hospital in French Equatorial Africa (now Gabon), directs his staff as a shipment of CARE blankets, shirts and clothing arrive in 1953. It marked the first time CARE sent aid to Africa. *(CARE photo by Erica Anderson)*

ABOVE: Carpentry students in Patras, Greece, examine the tools in a CARE woodworker's kit sent to their vocational school in 1957. Including tools in CARE Packages was the agency's first step toward addressing the larger issues of poverty. The "self-help" message was popular among American donors, who sent thousands of sturdy tool kits overseas. In 1994, a CARE relief worker in the former Yugoslavia met a carpenter who was still using a right angle that he received from CARE as a young man in 1954. *(CARE photo)*

ABOVE: A boy in Sri Lanka enjoys a CARE school lunch. In the 1950s and '60s, CARE began using surplus U.S. government food to improve nutrition in the developing world.

(CARE photo)

CARE and the Peace Corps

Perhaps the best-known development organization in the world is the Peace Corps, whose young American volunteers have worked side by side with the developing world's poor for 35 years. What few people know is that the Peace Corps, established by President John F. Kennedy, got started with significant help from CARE.

In the summer of 1961, CARE staff screened the first Peace Corps applicants and trained the first 125 volunteers in a grueling 16-hour-a-day program at Rutgers University in New Jersey. Only half the class completed the training and became America's first Peace Corps volunteers in 1961. They flew to Colombia, where CARE organized the first Peace Corps development project. Volunteers built roads, dug wells, suggested improvements for village sanitation and worked to increase farm yields.

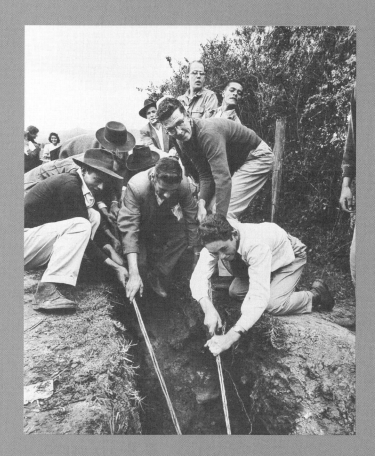

The first Peace Corps volunteers, trained by CARE, help construct a well in Colombia in 1961. *(CARE photo)*

CARE's formal involvement with the Peace Corps ended in 1967, but many Peace Corps alumni have worked for CARE over the years, and volunteers are still occasionally assigned to CARE projects.

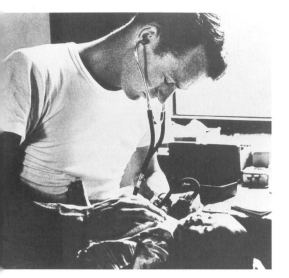

LEFT: Dr. Tom Dooley, the co-founder of MEDICO, treats a child in Laos in the late 1950s. CARE's affiliation with MEDICO, which sent physicians overseas to run clinics and provide medical training, made health care a bigger part of its overseas operations. *(CARE photo)*

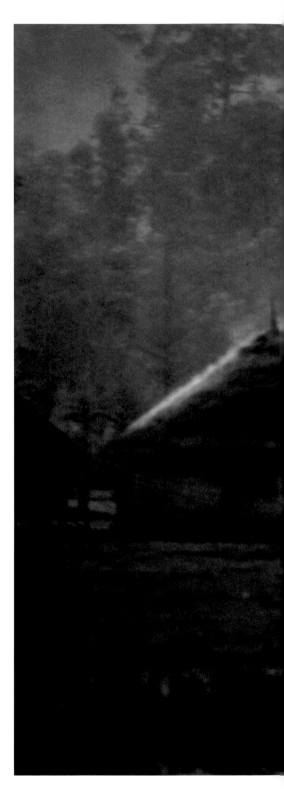

LEFT: A woman in Ecuador draws water from a well that her village built with help from CARE in 1969, when CARE began working with communities to build schools, water systems and other improvements. *(CARE photo)*

Working to benefit entire villages, like this one in Ethiopia, became a growing part of CARE's work during the 1970s and '80s. *(CARE photo by Scott Faiia)*

Nutrition, Education and Unforeseen Gains

It was devised as a straightforward CARE school-lunch program to help improve nutrition for children in a remote corner of India. It became, instead, the "Tamil Nadu miracle," a case study in how educating girls can lead to dramatic social benefits.

"It was basically promoted on the belief that the children were

undernourished and would be better students if they had a free midday meal," recalls Philip Johnston, who managed the program as a young development worker in the 1960s and went on to become CARE's president. "Still, we suspected that the program would also lure more children into the classroom."

The suspicion was correct. Parents who had kept their daughters at home to do chores began sending them to school to eat the free meals and bring food home to share. Once they were in the classroom, however, the children received more than food.

A school lunch program in India in 1960. *(CARE photo)*

"The children learned to read, and literacy made it possible for them to understand the messages of family planning and birth spacing," says Johnston. "Later, as they began to marry, they applied the messages to their lives."

Birthrates in the state dropped 25 percent from 1971 to 1991, while increased literacy also contributed to gains in women's income and the health of their children. In 1995, CARE established a girls' education program, recognizing that women's literacy is a key to reducing poverty.

ABOVE: In the mountains of Honduras, a toddler gets a bath in 1992. In a partnership typical of CARE water projects, the villagers supplied all the labor and part of the funding themselves, and continue to pay for its upkeep and maintenance.

(Photo © 1992 by Tony Arruza)

ABOVE: Clean and plentiful water helps reduce the spread of waterborne diseases. A CARE well came to this village in Cameroon in 1982. Since the end of World War II, access to reliable water has increased from 10 percent to 60 percent in rural areas worldwide.

(CARE photo by H. Shaw McCutcheon)

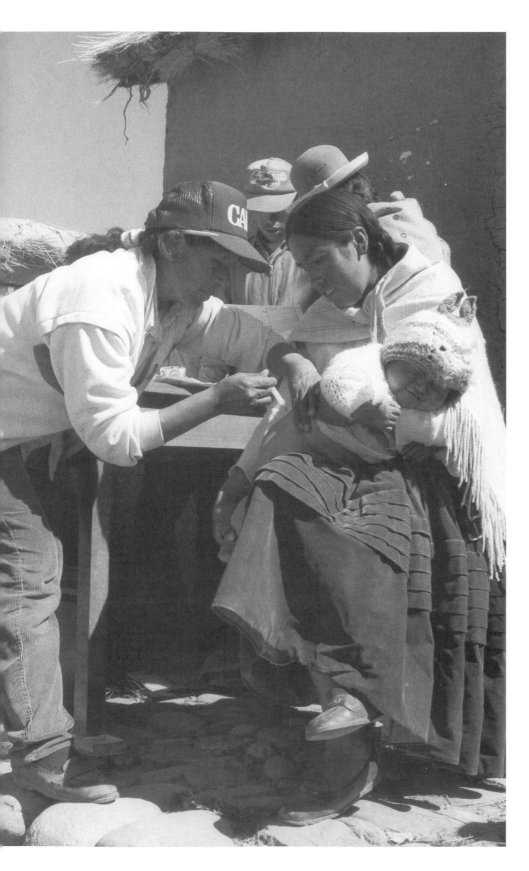

ABOVE: A girl in Mali is a bit wary of being next in line for oral polio vaccine in 1988. In the 1980s, immunization rates jumped from 15 to 80 percent in many developing nations, saving an estimated three million lives each year. Oral-rehydration therapy, a low-cost way to stop deadly diarrhea, also became widespread during the 1980s, saving another one million lives annually. *(CARE photo by Annie Pringle)*

ABOVE: A Bolivian baby grimaces as he receives an immunization from a CARE-trained health worker in 1988. The program is typical of the preventive health programs that CARE began in the 1970s. *(CARE photo by Carolyn Watson)*

A CARE-trained health worker meets with a mother in Bangladesh. Training village health workers in simple preventive practices has proved a low-cost means of improving the health status of poor households. *(CARE photo by Shahidul Alam)*

ABOVE: A woman in Ethiopia makes her living in the marketplace. CARE began helping people start and expand small businesses in the 1980s by providing small loans, business training and help in marketing goods and creating savings. *(CARE photo by Scott Faiia)*

ABOVE: More than half of all participants in CARE small business programs are women, like this grocer in Sri Lanka, who received a small loan and was able to open her shop. *(CARE photo by David Morris)*

LEFT: A carpenter in Chad who received small-business assistance from CARE in 1985. Credit is often difficult to obtain for the poor in developing nations; a loan of $50 or less can provide the opportunity for a more secure economic future. *(CARE photo by H. Shaw McCutcheon)*

ABOVE: Farmers in Bangladesh, where a high population density means that all available land must be used for rice production. *(CARE photo by Rudolph von Bernuth)*

In the 1990s, CARE has focused attention on population programs, recognizing that the absence of family-planning services is a serious obstacle to the health and economic well-being of poor families. ABOVE: In Peru, a CARE-trained family-planning officer visits a young mother. RIGHT: In Bangladesh, a nurse checks the blood pressure of a woman at a family planning clinic supported by CARE. Having fewer children leaves more resources for health, education, housing and food, and improves the health of both mothers and children. Family-planning programs have helped slow population growth in developing nations by one-third since 1971, easing the population burden on poor countries and the global environment. *(CARE photos)*

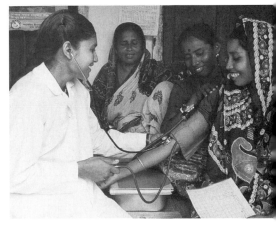

ABOVE: The global AIDS epidemic has hit developing nations particularly hard. In northern Thailand, CARE is helping this 28-year-old mother, who is HIV-positive, and others find work, while encouraging family members and the communities to accept and care for AIDS patients. *(CARE photo by Katya Andresen)*

RIGHT: In Kenya, CARE, with funding from the Starbucks Coffee Company, produces a comic book for school children that addresses environmental and health issues, including AIDS.

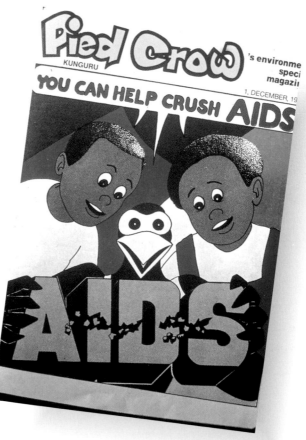

Renewing a Worn-out Land

Wichai Wonsunrasombat, a farmer in northern Thailand, remembers a time when he could not grow enough food to feed his wife and three children. To survive, he went to work in town after spending long days in his own fields. But then, in 1984, CARE came to his mountain village to help 9,000 families of the Karen hill tribe, one of Thailand's poorest, most remote ethnic groups.

Wichai and other members of the tribe had suffered years of declining crop yields because of unsustainable slash-and-burn agricultural practices that left farmland exhausted and razed vast swaths of forest. Fertilizers and insecticides did

Shown here in 1989, Wichai binds coconut fiber around the branch of a mango tree. Once bound, such branches sprout roots and can be cut and planted to produce another fruit tree. *(CARE photo by John Everingham)*

little to help. But CARE offered new and more affordable solutions.

Rotating crops and growing soybeans added nutrients to the soil. Planting fruit trees slowed erosion and yielded nutritious food. Pest-resistant seeds reduced the need for chemical insecticides. Gradually, Wichai's land and that of his neighbors began to recover, producing soybeans, rice, mangoes and something Wichai once thought was quite impossible: a surplus.

ABOVE AND UPPER RIGHT: In Nepal (above), a farmer works in his vegetable garden. *(CARE photo by Scott Faiia)* **Ethiopian women (upper right) tend to the tree seedlings they will later plant as a source of firewood and animal fodder and as a means of erosion control.** *(CARE photo by Santha Faiia)* **CARE began helping farmers find more productive and environmentally sound ways to grow food in the 1970s. The work was greatly expanded in the 1980s, as CARE encouraged farmers to use natural pesticides, plant trees to halt soil erosion and stop destructive slash-and-burn farming methods. In Nicaragua, CARE helped reduce pesticide use by 80 percent without a loss of crop yield.**

ABOVE: Children in Bangladesh. Future generations will inherit the world, and the resources, we leave behind. *(CARE photo by Rudolph von Bernuth)*

The CHALLENGE AHEAD

Education holds the
promise of a better
future for these girls in
a classroom in Mali.
*(CARE photo by Michel
Dompierre)*

The world 50 years from now will in all likelihood resemble our own era even less than today resembles the days of Harry Truman and hungry children on the streets of Europe. The pace of change is ever-increasing, bringing new problems and new opportunities—many of which cannot be anticipated. Some of the challenges ahead, however, are already in focus because they arise from two interlocking causes that trouble the world today: the huge and growing gap between the world's rich and poor, and the reckless depletion of the earth's natural resources.

The wealthiest 20 percent of people on earth receive 82 percent of income; the poorest 20 percent receive about one percent. The poorest of the poor account for 1.3 billion people, and another 500 million will join their ranks in the next 15 years. Meanwhile, 850 million people already live in environmentally fragile areas, where their efforts to survive often exacerbate soil erosion, deforestation and the loss of natural habitats. At the same time, industrialized countries, competing intensely for new markets and economic growth, continue to consume natural resources and produce waste at unsustainable levels.

All of these economic and environmental trends are likely to continue in the decades ahead. Looked at through the most pessimistic of prisms, the near future is a place where more of the very poor will endure more economic injustice amid fewer natural resources. It is hardly a recipe for social stability, and the growing number of armed conflicts worldwide can be traced in part to these emerging realities.

In this climate, CARE approaches the new millennium with an awareness of the sobering reality that more people than ever will need its services, even as it adapts its programs to a changing world. And so, as it marks the passage of 50 years, CARE is continuing the search for solutions.

One conclusion is already certain: The threats arising from global poverty will not be confined to the developing world. Environmental degradation, population growth, the global AIDS epidemic, war and refugee crises, economic instability—each has global dimensions that affect people everywhere.

Some solutions can be found in the lessons of the past. Fifty years of work in 125 countries has provided CARE with a deep well of experience from which to draw. These lessons are helping to shape a new agenda for CARE's work, in which programs will focus more sharply on the poorest of the poor, especially women and children, and their most critical needs: a secure environment, basic health and population services, economic opportunity and education, relief and rehabilitation. More programs will reach out to the urban poor, in response to the phenomenal growth of urban populations in the developing world. Success in meeting this agenda will be measured not by how much food is delivered or how many trees are planted but by the tangible and sustainable impact on individual households. Finally, CARE will rely more than ever on partnerships with indigenous groups in poor countries, helping them to hone their own capacity to address social and economic needs while making CARE's programs more efficient.

As CARE looks to the future, it is worth noting that the men and women who founded the organization in 1945 scarcely imagined that their creation would grow into an enduring American institution. Most, in fact, figured that CARE would close up shop before the decade was over. Even Paul Comly French, CARE's tireless early leader, wrote in 1948: "From every indicator in the light of discussions I had with government ministers, industrialists, labor leaders and newspapermen, it seems likely to me that the fall and winter of 1948-49 will be the last winter in which CARE's services will be needed."

The lesson is that time and events will bring changes never imagined; but that a mission to help the world's poor—based on compassion, yet grounded in practical approaches—can be as relevant in the future as it has been in the past.

ABOVE: Farmers work their fields in the highlands of Peru as a storm approaches. They rank among the one billion people on earth who earn less than $1 a day. *(Photo © 1993 by J.F. Housel)*

RIGHT: Villagers in Niger carry firewood across the desert. Growing populations and dwindling natural resources are forcing more and more of the world's poor to live in environmentally fragile areas. *(CARE photo by Susan Bailey)*

ABOVE: In the sprawling slums of Lima, Peru, a woman carries home water, an increasingly precious resource as populations grow. Many women spend two or more hours a day walking to and from water sources—time they could spend increasing their incomes, learning to read, caring for their children. *(Photo © 1993 by J.F. Housel)*

ABOVE: A boy in Honduras carries firewood past a field being cleared by burning. The rate of tropical-forest destruction worldwide is equivalent to about one soccer field per second as people clear land for farming, firewood and other uses. *(Photo © 1992 by Tony Arruza)*

ABOVE: Just up the road from the scene of destruction shown at left, Jose Isai Medina, at age nine, is finding solutions. CARE extension agents helped the Honduran boy's father find environmentally sound alternatives to slash-and-burn farming. *(Photo © 1992 by Tony Arruza)*

Farmers in Peru. Using the earth's resources wisely and fairly will be the major challenge of the 21st century.
(Photo © 1993 by J.F. Housel)

ABOVE: In Sudan, a well built with CARE's help is helping a village rebuild after civil war. *(CARE photo by H. Shaw McCutcheon)*

LEFT: In southern Sudan, years of civil conflict have made the weapons of war a familiar icon. *(Photo © 1994 by Yael Swerdlow)*

ABOVE: Children push their belongings through the streets of Kabul, Afghanistan, one of many nations where armed conflict is forcing children to grow up in a war zone. *(CARE photo by David Stewart Smith)*

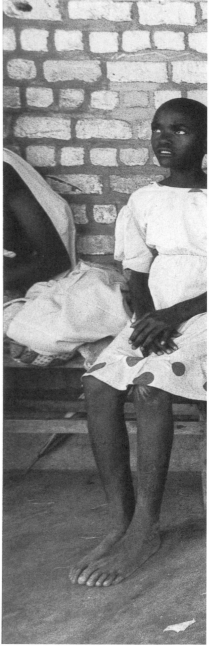

ABOVE: Enis Bogucanin, 16, was shot by a sniper in Sarajevo, where CARE is helping Bosnians recover from four years of war. Women, children and the elderly often suffer most in the ethnic conflicts that have proliferated in the 1990s. Defending their human rights and helping them recover from trauma will challenge the international community in the years ahead. *(Photo © 1995 by Jack Picone)*

ABOVE: Children in Rwanda in 1994, months after the explosion of ethnic violence that claimed half a million lives. *(Photo © 1994 by Yael Swerdlow)*

RIGHT: A child in the Philippines. Meeting the health and nutrition needs of the next generation of children will challenge the capacity of developing-world governments.
(Photo © 1993 by J.F. Housel)

Women in Mali carry home water. Working more closely with women—who work longer hours for less pay than men and bear the burden of raising children—is an important part of the development agenda for the next 50 years. *(CARE photo by Mark Stover)*

ABOVE: In Thailand, 15-year-old Wasana Pungpob works 12-hours a day to help support her family. A loan and training from CARE helped her increase her income.
(CARE photo by Khun Niwat)

ABOVE: Small business, family planning and girls' education programs will help women take greater control over their lives and futures in the years ahead.
(CARE photo by Mark Stover)

BELOW: Children study in a Honduran classroom. Many families in the developing world send their sons—but not their daughters—to school. Of the 100 million children between ages six and 11 who don't attend school, two-thirds are girls. Girls who do attend school are likely to earn more money, have fewer children and raise healthier families. Keeping girls in school is a major priority in the next 50 years. *(Photo © 1992 by Tony Arruza)*

Sisters in the Philippines. Countries that invest in the health and education of their children are rewarded with stronger economies and more stable societies than those that do not. *(Photo © 1994 by J.F. Housel)*

With its intense poverty and recent wave of genocide, Rwanda is a case study in the problems facing the most troubled developing nations in the years ahead. Still, despite an uncertain future, a fragile hope is alive. *(CARE photo by Christy Gavitt)*

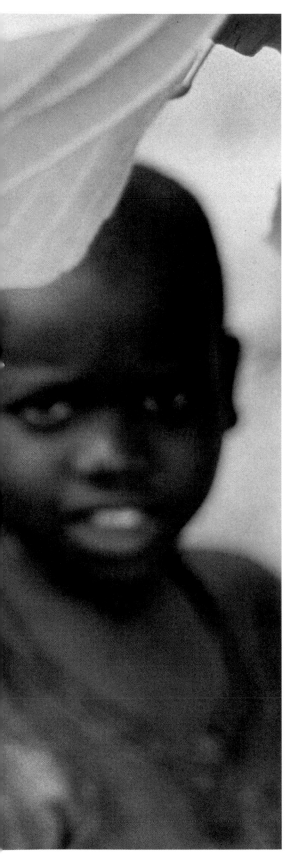

ABOVE: In the Amazon Basin of Peru, a CARE extension agent and a local farmer look for solutions to the natural-resource problems affecting the region. Solving the global problems ahead will demand a spirit of partnership between rich and poor, between north and south, between competing idealogies, between ethnic and religious rivals. *(Photo © 1993 by J.F. Housel)*

The FUTURE, THE CHILDREN

Peru, 1993.
(Photo © 1993 by J.F. Housel)

All we know about the future with any degree of certainty is the names of the people who will live in it: our children.

Since CARE was founded, helping children has been at the heart of its mission. Many programs—such as immunizations, school lunches and girls' education—directly involve children. Programs like these have dramatically reduced child mortality in the developing world, from 280 deaths per 1,000 live births in 1950 to 106 per 1,000 in 1990. And oral-rehydration therapy, a low-tech treatment for diarrhea, is saving the lives of one million children a year. Many other CARE programs indirectly help children by enabling their parents to grow more food, increase their income or better manage their natural resources.

And yet inequities remain between the children in industrialized countries and their counterparts in developing nations. In Africa, almost a third of the children under age five are undernourished. Every minute, a newborn in the developing world dies of a tetanus infection. Entirely preventable conditions—diarrheal disease, respiratory infection, malaria and malnutrition—kill nearly seven million children every year in developing countries. And in South Asia and South America, half of all children will leave school before fifth grade.

Meanwhile, new threats are making growing up harder. In

Africa, AIDS will orphan an estimated nine million children in the 1990s. Worldwide, children account for many of the world's 50 million refugees, and are among the most vulnerable to war, ethnic cleansing and land mines.

Solving all of these problems and putting children first on the world's agenda are both possible and affordable. In a world that spends more than a trillion dollars each year on the military, illegal drugs and cigarettes, the resources exist to provide every child with basic health care and 12 years of schooling. Investing in the well-being of children is not only a moral issue; it is a key to economic and social development. Countries that have made the choice to nurture the next generation have created more prosperous, stable and equitable societies. It is a question of priorities.

Over the years, photographs, film footage and video images of children have motivated generations of CARE donors to support the organization. People are not only moved by the horrific images of starvation but by the poignancy of a child across oceans, time zones and a seemingly vast cultural and economic divide acting remarkably like the child from across the street. Eating a bowl of soup. Holding a baby sister. Stomping in a puddle. Crying when it thunders. Sleeping in a mother's arms. There is a universality in children that reminds us that we are more alike than different, more united than

ABOVE: Germany, 1948.
(CARE photo)

divided and perhaps more capable than we imagined of living together on the same planet in relative peace and harmony.

The people who support CARE and those who participate in its programs share a desire to leave the world better than they found it. They reject the notion that poverty and the crushing weight it puts on children is an inevitable consequence of economic life. Instead, they work to make the future more promising—for their children, and for all children.

RIGHT: Bangladesh, 1988.
(CARE photo by Ahmed Munir)

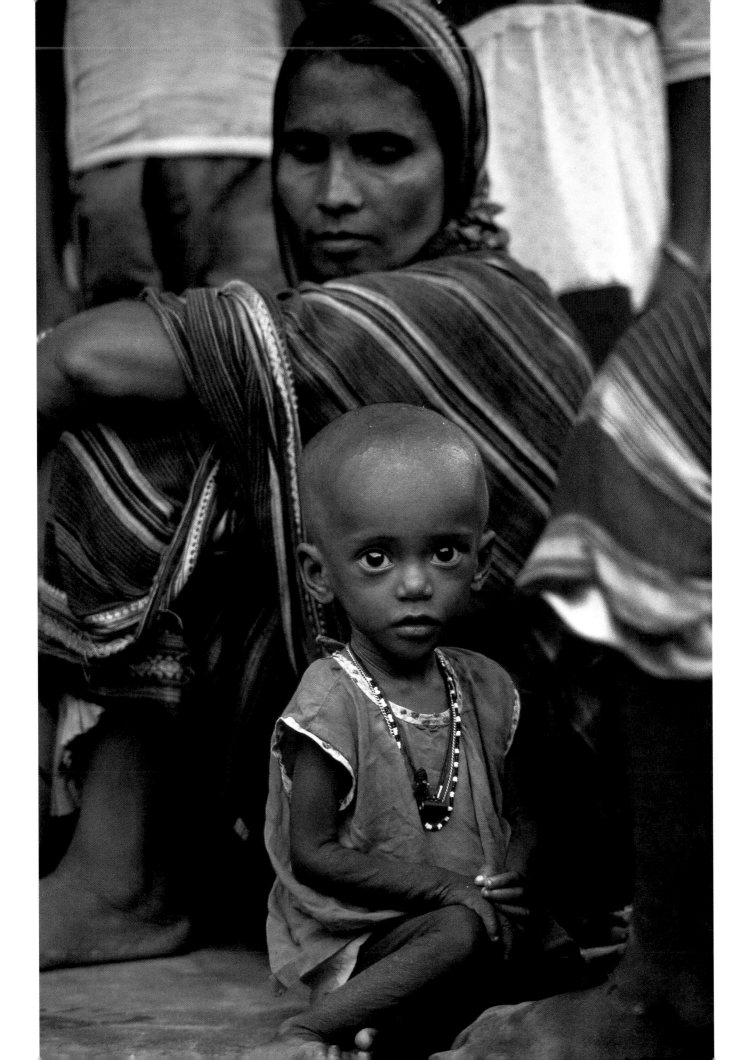

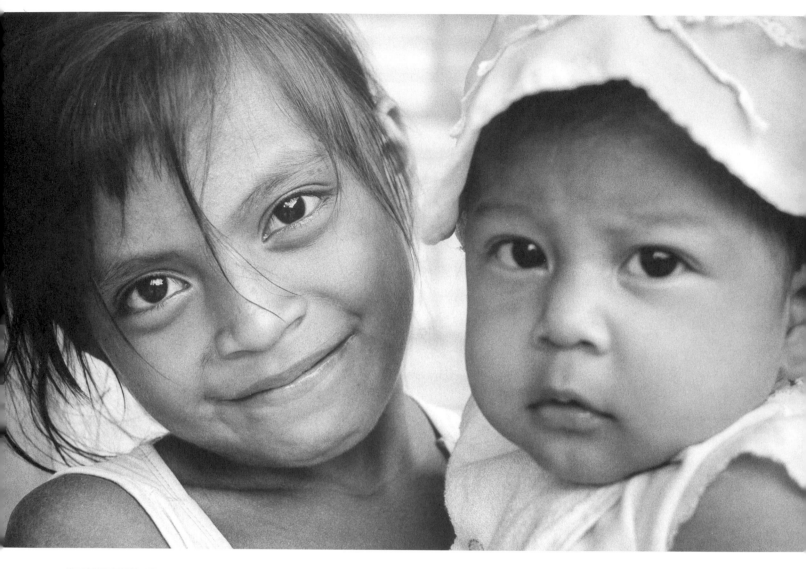

ABOVE: Philippines, 1994.
(Photo © 1994 by J.F. Housel)

LEFT: Nepal, 1993. *(CARE photo by Scott Faiia)*

Lesotho, 1985. *(CARE photo by Rudolph von Bernuth)*

ABOVE: Lesotho, 1985. *(CARE photo by Rudolph von Bernuth)*

ABOVE: Peru, 1993. *(Photo © 1993 by J.F. Housel)*

Philippines, 1994. *(Photo © 1994 by J.F. Housel)*

LEFT: Hungary, 1956.

(CARE photo)

LEFT: Sudan, 1984. *(CARE photo by Rudolph von Bernuth)*

RIGHT: Cambodia, 1979.

(CARE photo)

LEFT: Guatemala, 1995. *(CARE photo by Lisa Swenarski de Herrera)*

RIGHT: Vietnam, 1975.

(CARE photo by Kerry Heubeck)

ABOVE: Colombia, 1958. *(CARE photo)*

ABOVE: Korea, 1970.

(CARE photo)

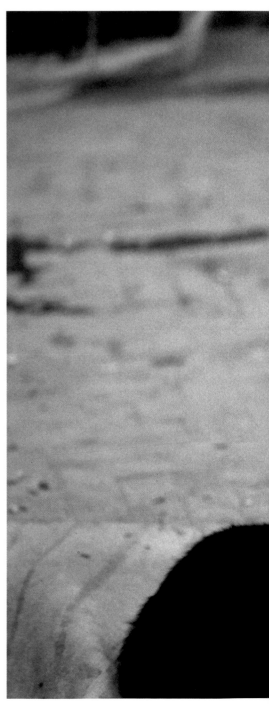

RIGHT: Nepal, 1986. *(CARE photo by Rudolph von Bernuth)*

RIGHT: Honduras, 1992.

(Photo © 1992 by Tony Arruza)

Honduras, 1992. *(Photo © 1992 by Tony Arruza)*

LEFT: Ecuador, 1990. *(CARE photo by Matthew De Galan)*

BELOW: Rwanda, 1994. *(CARE photo by Wendy Driscoll)*

ABOVE: India, 1995. *(CARE photo by Katya Andresen)*

LEFT: Peru, 1984. *(CARE photo by H. Shaw McCutcheon)*

RIGHT: Ecuador, 1981. *(CARE photo)*

Honduras, 1992. *(Photo © 1992 by Tony Arruza)*

AFTERWORD

AFTER 50 YEARS OF SERVICE, CARE HAS PERHAPS EARNED A MOMENT FOR REFLECTION. ACCOMPLISHMENTS ARE WORTHY OF CELEBRATION, AND THAT IS ONE PURPOSE OF THIS BOOK, AND ONE PURPOSE OF CARE'S 50TH ANNIVERSARY OBSERVANCE. AT CARE, HOWEVER, WE CANNOT AFFORD TO REST UPON OUR LAURELS. AS LONG AS POVERTY AND ITS BRUTAL EFFECTS HAUNT OUR WORLD, WE MUST CONTINUE TO WORK, SEEKING AND APPLYING NEW AND BETTER APPROACHES TO THE PROBLEMS THAT CONFRONT IMPOVERISHED PEOPLE ACROSS THE GLOBE.

I believe these problems can be solved. My faith comes, in part, from the many successes of the past 50 years. Infant mortality in the developing world declined by more than 50 percent between 1960 and 1992. The percentage of rural families with access to safe drinking water has climbed from a scant 10 percent in 1945 to 60 percent today. And primary school enrollment rose from 48 percent in 1960 to 78 percent in 1994. These are but a few success stories, and each has changed the lives of hundreds of millions of people. CARE is proud to have been a part of this progress.

But today there are new challenges ahead. Continued progress depends on the willingness of people everywhere to engage with the rest of the world. This doesn't mean simply supporting CARE (though it's a good place to start). It means taking a global view of problems, solutions and opportunities. The global economy is already a reality; corporations regard themselves as transnational entities that must appeal to a worldwide consumer audience. All of us must do no less. In what we buy, whom we vote for, how we invest, where we volunteer, how we live and what we care about, we must ask ourselves how our actions affect the larger world—and the future our children and their children will live in. We must recognize, for example, that saving the environment doesn't just mean urging Brazilians to stop cutting down rainforests; it means reducing consumption and pollution in the industrialized world and helping poor nations find economic alternatives to natural resource depletion. It means changing the way we live, and working with others as partners.

Finding solutions to such problems will be difficult, and sometimes costly. Thinking globally is one thing. Making the commitments and sacrifices that logically follow is quite another. We must, however, keep the rewards of success front and center: a world with a stable population and a secure environment. A world where food finds its way to the hungry. A world where basic education brings economic opportunity. A world where conflicts are resolved peacefully and human and civil rights are respected.

All of this is possible. But it will take all of us to make it happen. At CARE, we have seen the progress that results from human beings working together for change against great odds and the most trying circumstances. This gives us an optimism that some may regard as naive. We prefer to view it as wisdom—a wisdom gained from witnessing humanity at its best and worst, and knowing which force is ultimately stronger.

Peter D. Bell
President, CARE USA

Peter D. Bell visits with children outside a church in southwestern Rwanda in January 1996. (*CARE photo by Katharine Day Bremer*)

The World of CARE

Since 1946, CARE has worked in 125 countries on five continents

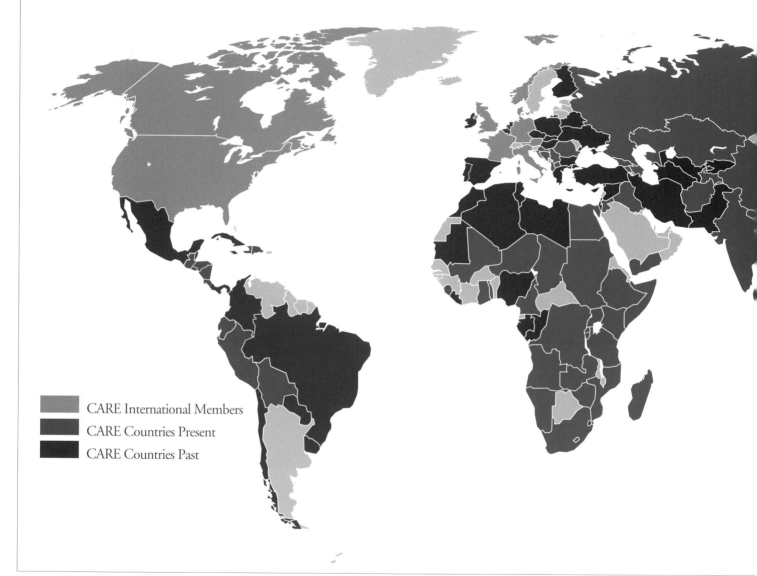

CARE International Members
CARE Countries Present
CARE Countries Past

India 1950-present
Indonesia 1967-present
Japan 1948-55
Korea 1948-79
Laos 1954-57, 1991-present
Macao 1955-59
Malaysia 1963-70
Nepal 1978-present
Okinawa 1948-55
Pakistan 1949-81
Papua New Guinea 1991-present
Philippines 1949-present
Singapore 1954
Sri Lanka 1950, 1956-present
Thailand 1950, 1979-present
Vietnam 1954-75, 1990-present

LATIN AMERICA

Belize 1962-93
Bolivia 1953-60, 1976-present
Brazil 1953-55
Chile 1953-55, 1960-85
Colombia 1954-84
Costa Rica 1957-present
Cuba 1959
Dominican Republic 1962-present
Ecuador 1951-present
El Salvador 1955-58, 1978-80, 1993-
   present
Guatemala 1958-present
Haiti 1953-56, 1959-present
Honduras 1954-present
Jamaica 1987-88
Mexico 1952-65, 1985-92
Nicaragua 1954-55, 1966-present
Panama 1953-89
Paraguay 1954-55
Peru 1952-55, 1957-58, 1970-present
Uruguay 1954-55

AFRICA

Algeria 1963-70
Angola 1990-present
Burundi 1993-present
Cameroon 1978-present
Chad 1974-present
Comoros 1984-present
Congo 1979-87
Egypt 1954-68, 1974-present
Ethiopia 1984-present
French Equatorial Africa 1953
Ghana 1995-present
Kenya 1968-present
Lesotho 1968-present

Liberia 1961-83
Libya 1955-65
Madagascar 1991-present
Mali 1975-present
Mauritania 1984-87
Morocco 1953-54
Mozambique 1984-present
Namibia 1994-present
Niger 1973-present
Nigeria 1968-76
Rwanda 1984-present
Sierra Leone 1961-present
Somalia 1981-present
South Africa 1993-present
Sudan 1979-present
Swaziland 1987-92
Tanzania 1994-present
Togo 1987-present
Tunisia 1950, 1962-83
Uganda 1969-73, 1979-present
Zaire 1995-present
Zambia 1992-present
Zimbabwe 1992-present

**CARE International Members
(and date of founding)**

CARE USA—1945
CARE Canada—1946
CARE Germany—1980
CARE Norway—1980
CARE France—1983
CARE Italy—1984
CARE United Kingdom—1985
CARE Austria—1986
CARE Japan—1987
CARE Australia—1987
CARE Denmark—1988

NOTE: *Seven CARE International member nations—Germany, France, the United Kingdom, Italy, Austria, Norway and Japan—also received aid from CARE after World War II. They are shown on the map as CARE International members, rather than former CARE countries.*

Palestinian Territories 1994-present
Syria 1953
Tajikistan 1992, 1994-present
Turkey 1959-79
Turkmenistan 1992
Uzbekistan 1992
Yemen 1993-present

ASIA

Bangladesh 1971-present
Burma 1950
Cambodia 1954, 1973-75, 1980-83,
   1991-present
China 1988-present
Hong Kong 1954-79

ACKNOWLEDGMENTS

IN LATE 1956, THE NEW MANAGER OF CARE'S PHOTOGRAPHY UNIT CALLED A YOUNG TYPIST INTO HER OFFICE AND GAVE HIM THE FOLLOWING INSTRUCTIONS: SIFT THROUGH THE ENTIRE PHOTOGRAPHIC COLLECTION, SELECT TWO PICTURES FROM EACH COUNTRY AND CARRY THE REST, BOX BY BOX, TO THE DUMPSTER. OPERATIONS ALL OVER EUROPE WERE CLOSING, THE MANAGER NOTED, AND A HANDFUL OF HISTORIC PICTURES WOULD BE MORE THAN ENOUGH FOR THE FUTURE.

The typist, fresh out of high school and eager to please, was loath to disregard the order. Yet he could not obey. Instead, he turned to a colleague, Jim Stasney, who came up with an alternative—a hiding place. Together, after their bosses had gone home, they moved five large filing cabinets packed with photos to an empty room on the top floor of CARE's headquarters, then housed in a former brewery in Manhattan. A few months later, the manager moved on. The photographs were spared, and the task of organizing the collection into a library fell to its rescuer— Pedro Soto. For the next 40 years, he built CARE's photo library into an unparalleled resource, with at least 500,000 images from 125 countries. These images have introduced generations of Americans to CARE's work and to the people of the developing world. Today, Pedro is still at it, nurturing the collection like a proud father, tirelessly pursuing compelling images of new projects. CARE staffers, year after year, have marveled at his ability to find a photograph among the dozens of filing cabinets with

only the sparsest of clues—*a little girl with a bow in her hair eating a bowl of soup, maybe in India.* Before the description is finished, he smiles, turns quickly, pulls open a drawer and hands over the print.

Needless to say, without Pedro, this book would not exist.

Many fine photographers have contributed to the CARE photo library over the years. In the early days, mission chiefs hired local photographers, many of whom were superb European photographers desperate for work. CARE staffers have contributed to the library as well, and most of the images in this book are their work. Some are accomplished photographers, such as Scott Faiia, a veteran country director, and Rudolph von Bernuth. Many professional photographers have also helped CARE tell its story. J.F. Housel, a Seattle photographer, deserves special mention. Each year he travels, at his own expense, to a CARE project to document the organization's work. His work appears throughout this book; its quality, and his commitment, speak for themselves.

Turning these photographs, and

the history they portray, into a book was the work of many dedicated people. Matthew De Galan is the editorial director of this book and a CARE staffer since 1988. Over the past two years, he coordinated the research on CARE's history, developed the concept for this book and shaped its editorial and creative direction. Assisting him throughout this process was Erin Blair, who tirelessly tracked down and interviewed more than 100 CARE Package recipients. Our link to the past was Peg Ford Taska, who began working for CARE in 1946 and became CARE's historian even before she retired. Her insight and keen memory were invaluable.

Several other CARE staff members have helped bring this book into being through their support and their thoughtful contributions, including: Katharine Day Bremer, senior vice president/marketing; Marc M. Lindenberg, senior vice president/program; Pierre Ferrari, special assistant to the president; Guy Arledge, director of communications; Tony Williams, creative services manager; and Jennifer Dunlap, vice president of the CARE Foundation.

Dr. Philip Johnston, now president of the CARE Foundation, deserves special mention for the central role he has played in CARE history. As a student volunteer at Northeastern University, as an overseas worker and, finally, as CARE's president, he has served the less-fortunate of our world with passion and distinction.

The people at Longstreet Press, and especially the president, Chuck Perry, also merit high praise. Organizational histories are hardly a hot publishing property. But Longstreet saw that the real story was the rise of an American movement that had much to say about the world in the second half of the 20th century. Jill Dible's design brought the CARE story to life with sensitivity and a deep appreciation for the power of photography.

The final tribute for this book must go, however, to the four groups of people who collectively make CARE possible: the 10,000 staff members around the world, and the many thousands who have gone before them, who work in difficult, often dangerous conditions; the 48 million people in developing nations who work in partnership with CARE; the hundreds of thousands of donors worldwide, including individuals, corporations, governments and organizations; and, finally, the volunteer leaders of CARE's Board who made this book possible and embody the humanitarian spirit.

THE CARE BOARDS OF DIRECTORS AND OVERSEERS, 1996

BOARD OF DIRECTORS

Officers

Chair
Lydia M. Marshall
President
Peter D. Bell
Vice Chairs
Samuel E. Bunker
Ruth A. Wooden
Treasurer
Glenn H. Hutchins
Assistant Treasurer
Bruce C. Tully
Secretary
Lincoln C. Chen, M.D.
Assistant Secretary
Carol Andersen
(non-voting)
President Emeritus
Wallace J. Campbell

Members

Peter Ackerman, Ph.D
Managing Director
Rockport Capital, Inc.
Peter D. Bell
President, CARE
Samuel E. Bunker
Former Administrator,
International Programs Division,
National Rural Electric Cooperative
Association

Nancy S. Calcagnini
Former Managing Director
CS First Boston, Inc.
Lincoln C. Chen, M.D.
Taro Takemi Professor of
International Health
Harvard University School of
Public Health
W. Bowman Cutter III
Deputy Assistant to the President
for Economic Policy
National Economic Council
Jane C. Freeman
Former National President
Girl Scouts of America
Martha Hertelendy
Piedmont, California
Glenn H. Hutchins
Senior Managing Director
The Blackstone Group
Idriss Jazairy
Executive Director
A.C.O.R.D.
Mary Ellen Johnson
Former Vice President & Treasurer
Sara Lee Corporation
Peter H. Kaskell
Vice President
CPR Institute for Dispute
Resolution
Deborah Leff
President
Joyce Foundation

Whitney MacMillan
Director Emeritus
Cargill, Inc.
Lydia Micheaux Marshall
Executive Vice President
Sallie Mae
Gay Johnson McDougall
Executive Director
International Human Rights Law
Group
John Melcher
Former U.S. Senator
State of Montana
Timothy D. Proctor
SVP, General Counsel & Secretary
Glaxo Wellcome, Inc.
Merrill Rose
Executive Vice President
Porter/Novelli
Isabel Carter Stewart
National Executive Director
Girls Incorporated
Bruce C. Tully
Managing Director
Bankers Trust Company
Bertram E. Walls
President & CEO
Century American Insurance
Group
Ruth A. Wooden
President
The Advertising Council

BOARD OF OVERSEERS

Public Members

Charles H. Antholt
Senior Agriculturalist
The World Bank
William H. Foege, M.D., MPH
Fellow for Health Policy
The Carter Center
Robert W. Frelick, M.D.
Consultant on Chronic Diseases
Delaware Division of Public Health
Robert L. Gale
President Emeritus
Association of the Governing
Boards of Universities and Colleges
Edward H. Hoenicke
Former Senior Vice President &
General Counsel
United Airlines
Ralph Hofstad
President
Hofstad and Associates
Steven L. Isenberg
Former Deputy Publisher
Newsday
Maynard H. Jackson
Chairman of the Board
Jackson Securities
Richard P. Jones, Esquire
Former Law Secretary
New York State Supreme Court
David N. Pincus
Chairman & CEO
Pincus Brothers-Maxwell
John Rau
Dean, School of Business
Indiana University

Agustin Rivera
President
Global Education Initiatives
Edward A. Robie
Laconia, New Hampshire
Norman Ross
Former Senior Vice President
First Natioanl Bank of Chicago
Robert D. Scherer
President
AGLANDS, Inc.
David J. Scholes
President & CEO
Rapp Collins Worldwide
Douglas V. Siglin
Deputy Director
of Congressional Relations
The Nature Conservancy
Paul Spray, M.D.
Orthopaedic Surgeon
Methodist Medical Center
of Oak Ridge
Harry W. Strachan
Director
Bain & Co.
Louis W. Sullivan, M.D.
President
Morehouse School of Medicine
Carl Ware
Group President, Africa Group
The Coca-Cola Company
Edwin J. Wesely
Senior Partner
Winthrop, Stimson, Putnam &
Roberts
M. Moran Weston, Ph.D.
Heathrow, Florida

Andrew H. Young
Vice Chairman
Law Companies Group, Inc.
Sally W. Yudelman
Senior Fellow
International Center
for Research on Women

Organizational Members & Delegates

American Federation of Labor
& Congress of Industrial
Organizations
Charles D. Gray
Baptist World Alliance
Paul Montacute
Credit Union National Assoc. Inc.
Pete Crear
Gen. Federation of Women's Clubs
Jeannine Faubion
International Rescue Committee
Edwin J. Wesely
Junior Chamber International
Benny Ellerbe
Land O' Lakes, Inc.
Martha M. Cashman
National Cooperative Business
Association
Russell C. Notar
National Council of State Garden
Clubs, Inc.
Nan Jean Roller
National Farmers Union
Leland Swenson
National Peace Corps Association
Charles F. Dambach
Tolstoy Foundation
Xenia Woyevodsky

(All Directors are also members of the Board of Overseers)